ENDORS~~~~

In this relatively short volume, Dr. Edward Vick presents a thorough and precise overview of the Christian doctrine of Creation. This book has enormous value as a stand alone text yet, when coupled with Herold Weiss' outstanding review of relevant Scriptural texts, provides theological insights which complement the task of Scriptural exegesis with respect to this important doctrine of Creation. There is no wasted word in this truly magnificent work as Dr. Vick explains and defines important terminology and challenges us to look at complex questions reasonably and faithfully. While its topic is creation, it would serve well as a primer in the relationship of faith, Scripture and theology, a relationship with practical applcability to a multiplicity of issues confronting modern Christianity. In short, this is an outstanding resource in Christian theology, one to which I expect to return many, many times.

Rev. Dr. Robert R. LaRochelle, Author, *Crossing the Street* and
Part Time Pastor, Full Time Church

For the truth-seeker who takes seriously both faith and science, this thoughtful book makes a lot of sense, especially as a follow-up to its companion volume by Herold Weiss (*Creation in Scripture*). I found the discussion questions on creation, and the conversation among three Christian friends, unique, provocative, and elucidating features of this masterful contribution to a vexed and timely topic.

Lawrence T. Geraty, President Emeritus
La Sierra University

Drawing from the history of the relevant developments in philosophy and theology, Vick presents a cogent argument for a confessional Christian doctrine of Creation. To this end he makes important distinctions and gives concrete definitions to the vocabulary needed for the task. He argues that scientific and historical understandings of how the reality in which we live came to be are religiously irrelevant. Instead he presents a Christian understanding of what a doctrine of creation affirms. The clarity of the presentation and the relevance of its message makes this a most welcome contribution to a debate that quite often lacks both. I highly recommend its careful reading to the layperson, the cleric and the professional theologian, be they either Christian or non-Christian.

Herold Weiss, author of *Creation in Scripture*
Professor Emeritus of New Testament, St. Mary's College
Notre Dame

CREATION:

THE CHRISTIAN DOCTRINE

EDWARD W. H. VICK

Energion Publications
Gonzalez, Florida
2012

Cover Design: Henry Neufeld
Cover Image: © Jorisvo I Dreamstime.com

ISBN10: 1-938434-02-1
ISBN13: 978-1-938434-02-0
Library of Congress Control Number: 2012943562

Energion Publications
P. O. Box 841
Gonzalez, FL 32560

energionpubs.com
850-525-3916

FOREWORD

This writing provides a systematic treatment of the topic of creation. Its companion examines what Biblical writings teach on the subject, written by a New Testament expert, my colleague, Dr. Herold Weiss.

A satisfactory Christian understanding of the doctrine of creation, as of any other doctrine, depends both on examining Scriptural teaching and also taking into account the results of thinking about the meaning of the theme as it has developed through the centuries of Christian thought and as it is now expounded.

Several wide-ranging changes have taken place since the emergence of Christian faith in the first century of our era. These have each in their turn and together influenced the understanding and expression of Christian doctrine, not least the doctrine of creation. Patterns of thought and culture develop from one period to another. Revolutions in thought occur and it makes a difference to our understanding of life and of the world when they do. You and I are neither ancient nor medieval in our thinking.

Concerned believers have always found that when they think about the meaning of the creation of the cosmos, they must reckon with the astonishing advances in our recent knowledge. Not least of these are those of the astronomers, pushing out the boundaries and presenting us with an almost incredibly vast and complicated universe.

I am happy to express my sincere thanks, to my friend Herold Weiss for continuing and constructive support, to Esther my wife for her interest and helpful suggestions as she read one draft after another, to Henry Neufeld for his patience and encouragement

I dedicate this writing to the memory of my devoted mother

IVY MARY VICK

lost after a prolonged illness bravely borne,
when I was twelve years old.

Her love and encouragement set the pattern for my life.

TABLE OF CONTENTS

PART I

INTRODUCTION

Where shall we start?

Our task and interest is to provide a Christian doctrine of creation. The obvious question will be: Since the world exists and there are various explanations of the beginning and continuing existence of the world in which we 'live and move and have our being', what is it that makes the Christian account different from others? Some accounts, even in a Christian context, are not Christian accounts. How does the Christian account differ from other theistic accounts where God is originator, or from non-theistic accounts, which explain the origin of all things without reference to a deity or a supreme being? In what way does a Christian account differ from a philosophical or a scientific one?

We are bound to recognise and acknowledge that many of these accounts are rational, authentic, and often very sophisticated. Some, we may find, are quite justified and independent of any Christian account we may give.

We may go a step further. Some non-Christian accounts may be of such a character that they may contribute, when duly formulated and considered, to the formation of an acceptable Christian statement. Other such accounts may be quite independent and authentic in their own right, but have nothing to contribute to a distinctively Christian account of creation.

An important consideration is about the starting point of our Christian presentation. Shall we attempt to go to the very edge of human history and — so to speak — try to transcend our limitations and stand with God before his creative act and contemplate the possibility that God must consider all possible alternatives and choose the very best world. Do we then say that that is what he has done? But is that a realm so remote from ours that we really cannot say anything about it? Remember God's question to Job, 'Where were you when I created the world?'

Since as Christians we have an authoritative Scripture to give us guidance in our thinking, shall we as far as we are able, project ourselves to the edge of human and material existence and discern the lone God issuing words of command that bring the universe into being, as the writer of *Genesis* portrayed it? Shall we assume we can go beyond our limits and question the mind of the Creator before and during the creative act? Or shall we start somewhere within what turned out to be a long and very sorry course of human history? If the latter, we shall take some particular events among the whole as indicating the meaning of it all. Then we may find the idea of creation to provide the proper and quite adequate medium for expressing that meaning. That point in human history is Jesus Christ. He is the Word who was at the beginning who 'became flesh and dwelt among us', who as the source of human fulfilment will be at the end. Viewed in this way, creation is, for the Christian, an eschatological theme. 'Beginning, mean and end of all things' God, the Word. The end, mean, and the beginning all focus on the Christ-event.

Christian faith provides the ground and the source for all Christian teaching. Before there can be Christian understanding there is Christian faith. Before there was any Christian writing and any acceptance of such writings, there was Christian faith. 'Theology' is the term we use for the deliberate attempt to understand the faith. The theologian takes faith as the given without which he could not understand. So an old and widely accepted definition of the theologian's task was given (by Anselm) as *fidens quaerens intellectum*, 'faith seeking understanding'. The believer (i.e. the person who has faith) seeks to give an account of the meaning of Christian faith, seeks to work out in his mind what faith involves.

So, what does not have to do with faith is not theology. What does not have to do with Christian faith is not Christian theology. The Anselmian definition of theology provides for the exclusion of all non-Christian understandings of Christian theology.

As a person of faith, the theologian lives at a particular time and in a particular place. These provide him with his context. Contexts change, often radically. With new contexts come new challenges to understand the faith in the light of those changes. As we reflect on the topic of change we recognise that there was a time when little was known about our world.

Some Terms Explained

It is well at this point that we provide a definition or two.

World may be used simply to mean planet earth, or it may mean the universe. Since the word 'world' is sometimes used of the universe, we have to distinguish between these two meanings 'world' meaning universe and 'world' meaning earth

Universe means all that exists.

Cosmos is derived by simple transliteration from the Greek *kosmos*. This word meant order, good arrangement. So it was used of the universe, which the Greeks knew to exemplify order. 'Cosmos' is the universe seen as an ordered system.

Cosmology: a theory of the universe and its laws. The term is derived from two Greek words: *cosmos*, world + *logos*, order, reason.

Cosmogony: an account of the generation of the universe. The term is derived from two Greek words: *cosmos*, world + *gonos*, offspring.

World-view means the understanding one has of the universe, including the place of the earth within the universe and including one's place within the whole. The term is sometimes used to mean a person's outlook on life, somewhat as the word 'philosophy' is loosely used in a similar way.

When relatively little was known about the structure of Earth, our world, and of its lace in the heavens, some cultures gave a rather simple explanation. Others, more sophisticated, were interested in the heavens. The earth fit into a system of heavenly bodies whose movements could be traced with great patience. Unfortunately, along the long road to understanding, much error was taken as truth. One world view dominated European thought for centuries. Unfortunately, that earth-centred view was mistaken.

We must now make other distinctions between the meaning of the following terms: theology, doctrine, dogma and biblical exegesis.

Christian communities are many and varied. Different churches have developed different teachings. They have summarised such accepted teachings and produced statements of doctrine in shorter creedal pronouncements.

Creed: A definitive statement of accepted beliefs.

Doctrine simply means 'teaching' and so comes to mean the teachings of the particular church.

Dogma means teaching that has become traditional and often unquestionable. The term sometimes has a negative connotation. Then it means that there can be no change, no questioning of the teaching so stated.

However the term does not always have that negative sense. It points to the working out in some detail of the teachings. So it may then be a synonym for 'theology'. Dogmatics is another synonym.

The term **theology** simply means exposition of the faith and the teachings dependent on that faith. It is theology because its subject matter is God, *theos*.

One further distinction is important. Biblical theology or **exegesis** concerns itself with the scriptural texts. The task is to understand and expound them. It provides analyses both of what the texts meant to the writers and readers, and also interprets what they can mean for us in our differing contexts. So we distinguish **biblical theology** from **systematic theology.**

This we can illustrate by reference to our theme, creation. On the one hand there is the exposition of the teaching of individual passages of Scripture, for example, of the first chapter of the Gospel of *John*; of single books, e.g. of the book of *Colossians,* and then a presentation of the teaching of the whole corpus, the New Testament.

We will approach our theme from two different angles. I say 'we' because this writing is one of two. This one provides a theological account of the Christian teaching. My colleague, Herold Weiss, provides the companion volume. His is an exposition of individual books of the Bible on the theme of creation. So with this complementary pair you have a concrete example of the different approaches of systematic theology and of biblical theology.

So a brief word about their relation. Biblical exegesis is not just a piece of ancient history. Its task is not simply to make clear what they said long ago nor even to explain what they meant. It is also concerned with finding a meaning for today, and also, a more demanding task sometimes, of doing in our time what those ancient writers did for their time, connecting Christian faith with current problems and ideas in a relevant way. It is to be making a connection between the two tasks, what the text meant and what it now means.

Bible and Doctrine

It is obvious that the churches, varied as they are, take scriptural statements to be authoritative for doctrine. How that connection between Scripture and doctrine is worked out varies from community to community and from one individual to another. So theology is always suggestive, not simply repetitive.

What is clear is that the many individual scriptural writings have very different contexts. There are so many different contexts of time place and culture. So we shall begin to understand the individual writings as we construct the setting in which each was written.

What is also clear is that there is an overall context in which all the books of the Bible were composed and compiled. This was the accepted world-view of the ancient world. Take any particular passage, any individual book, or the whole corpus of writings and all are produced in this context, however much individual contexts may have differed. So we have two aspects to consider when we ask how we form a doctrinal statement in relation to biblical teaching.

(1) What relevance does the particular teaching or teachings of the passage, the book or the collected teaching of the whole corpus of books if and when these can be discerned, have for the doctrine of creation? For example, when a writing is concerned with addressing a false teaching, can the reply that was then given be duly interpreted as relevant to a contemporary statement? In *Colossians,* the heretical teaching of the *pleroma* is repudiated when Jesus Christ is made the central theme. But the repudiation consists in its reinterpretation and the concept being given a new application. The new term now gets employed as a Christian term. The opposition's term is Christianised, made a means for expressing a Christian interpretation. In the process of reapplication the Christian vocabulary is enlarged and understanding progresses, even as the progress depends upon employing a term originally used in a system opposed to the Christian understanding. Progress is made in Christian understanding as new ideas and themes emerge from the church's contact with other than Christian philosophies and standpoints.

This provides a model for the theologian of today, who does in our day what *Colossians* was doing in its day. The process takes place over and over again as the Christian witness has continued through the centuries. One of the tasks of the Christian theologian today is to explain the meaning of Christian faith in the particular context of our contemporary world. That will continuously and progressively involve the knowledge of hitherto unnoticed and unknown concepts considered to be possibly relevant and illuminating.

It will be clear from what we have said that Christian witness, while including reference to and understanding of Scripture, does not consist in the simple repetition of passages. Nor does Christian theology consist in simply coordinating passages of Scripture because they seem to fit together on a particular theme, and then drawing conclusions from the resulting collection.

Christian theologians, and this includes all who make the effort to understand Christian faith, will often engage with others in discussion of issues outside the realm of Christian belief. But then they will not pretend, if they are wise and understanding, that this is being done in the name of faith. One can seriously engage in the apparent interest of one's religious beliefs with both scientist and philosopher, and of course with other Christians with different views. But then sometimes one should not pretend that the engagement is Christian theology.

The frequent discussion of the age of the earth, often involving die-hard defence of a particular position, is a case in point. There is no Christian position on this topic, certainly not one that can be set against the scientists' accounts. The Christian who wishes to give such an authentic account will be producing scientific or historical, but not theological, results. If he enters the discussion he will not pretend that it is theology or Christian doctrine, or even that it is required by his Christian faith. Indeed he will not pretend that it has anything to do with Christian faith.

If I believe in God's revelation in Jesus Christ, what difference could it possibly make how old the universe is? That is the basic mistake of the creationist who argues from an interpretation of a scriptural passage (namely the early chapters in *Genesis*) which he interprets quite in isolation from his Christian faith, and then proceeds to construct an alternative but unfortunately pseudo-scientific or pseudo-historical account.

(2) The overall context of the biblical writer is that of a universe very different from ours. The earth is the focus of attention, the centre of things, set between the sky, the heaven above and the underworld beneath. Teachings about creation, ascension, or the second coming are all set within the framework of this understanding of our world. Their cosmos was a very simple one.

For us the earth is a tiny speck in an incomprehensively large, expansive universe. What we are and where we are becomes smaller and smaller as the most highly sophisticated telescopes become outdated. So we will one day say to Hubble, 'Thanks for pushing out the boundaries. But with our new telescopes we are now going further than you can reach.'

What ten billion light years is I cannot begin to understand. I can't even understand that our closest star, apart from the sun is 24,000,000,000,000 miles distant from earth and that is a very small distance, a very small fragment of the size of the universe. But we do not speak in terms of miles, rather in light years. A light year is 5.8 trillion miles, 9.46 trillion kilometres. We are told that the most distant galaxies are ten billion light years distant. It is quite credible that the actual size of the universe is unknown.

Classical Treatments of Creation

Christian writers have produced many treatises on the theme of creation. Non-Christian writers have for many millennia given thought to the question of beginnings, to the problem of being and non-being. As a result, certain treatments have become classic, and consideration of them beneficial, even essential for an adequate understanding of the issues. The different treatments, some opposed to others, may be clearly distinguished. Clarity based on such differentiation is very desirable. Acknowledging that there are alternative understandings, what results if one kind is confused with another is that there will be needless misunderstandings and arbitrary oppositions.

For example, giving an account of the emergence of the physical world at its beginning and holding that that is what a doctrine of creation is all about is a serious mistake. Creation conceived as the initial production of the physical universe and its inhabitants is not, and may have little or no relevance for, a Christian doctrine of creation.

For example, having said nothing about the character of God in insisting that the world was created in six days, the creationist then proceeds to say that an explanation of the origin of the world in evolutionary terms is opposed to the creation by God and must be replaced by an alternative explanation of the origins of phenomena within the universe.

It may not be Christian to say that talk about creation must start with the physical world, and so with the account of the creation as found in *Genesis* taken as such, and to read that account as concerned exclusively with origins. It may not even have religious significance. To construe it as such puts it on a par, and so on a collision course, with scientific explanations of the universe and of human existence.

We can engage in discussion on different levels. Agreement and disagreement arise in the process. When I write and you read what I write about creation, you have the choice of alternatives: (1) Maintaining and stating claims and not seriously considering any alternative, indeed not looking for rational support for what you believe. (2) Making claims and finding arguments you believe help you in establishing and in recommending those claims. (3) Making claims, then considering the way in which those claims have been defended and opposed in the past and being ready to accept new positions. If you take this last course you may then be in a defensible position to decide which warrants further consideration and acceptance.

It is important to recognise that the propositions and the arguments considered in relation to claims about creation will have been repeated many times in the past. That means that certain clear conclusions will have been proposed and serious and plausible reasons given for them. There are classic treatments of the important issues. So, you cannot avoid carefully considering these if you are serious, lest you be considered ignorant, and your position immature.

Considering Alternative Views

So instead of engaging face to face, you read a book or an article. You come across the printed text. You then discover that the positions stated are not those you yourself have held. Then what do you do? Cast the book aside! Or, do you consider that the author is saying. 'Always give a seriously held and well stated view that is different from yours a good hearing, or in our case a good reading.' You think seriously about it. Of course the writing could be entertaining if written well. If written convincingly, it could be persuasive.

We engage our reason to produce and evaluate arguments and conclusions and we then realise that we are not the first to do so. We are engaged in logical considerations, and so we are inevitably involved in (what we now call) philosophy. We shall save ourselves from needless naiveté and mistakes if we consider what has been said in the past,

We can learn what to avoid from discussion of alternative presentations. Often, unless you consider alternatives you do not come to a satisfactory position. If you don't consider serious alternatives, how do you know that your position is the most worthy? How do you defend your position in view of alternatives unless you know what the alternatives are?

We shall briefly consider some serious treatments of the past and present for help in exploring the problem of creation. In this writing such references will be serious, if not extensive. What questions do both theologians and philosophers ask? Or, put in another way, 'What questions do believers in God as Creator and those who do not so believe ask? What questions do they have in common?' If we can identify some of these, we can then ask whether the one can learn from the other, or whether it is a question of 'we' and 'they'.

We can learn from the history of Christian thinking over the centuries. For Christians have been very willing to read, digest, adjust to, and employ the concepts and conclusions from writers outside the realm of their particular theistic interests. At various times, Christians have been prepared to adopt the method of the thinkers and set their discussion in Christian terms, as seemed appropriate. Christians have been indebted for their understanding of creation to such sources.

Three sections

This book is divided into three parts. Each has its own style and function. The first part presents an introductory statement about how we approach a doctrinal explanation of the theme of creation. Then we give a theological account of the meaning of the assertion that God is Creator. For clarity's sake, we have already distinguished a systematic from a biblical treatment of the topic.

The second part presents statements by representative respected theologians as they expound the theme and argue for a separation of theology from science. It presents some quite basic positions.

We do not want to clutter the earlier sections with repeated arguments. But we do want, nonetheless, to present the issues involved when the subject of creation is raised with creationists and their literalist interpretations. So, the third section is in the form of a conversation — an effective way of introducing differing points of view, pro and con.

The style in the different sections differs. The argument of the whole is a unity.

Preliminary Brief Statement of the Christian Doctrine

We now, in this introductory chapter, present in brief statements, the main features of the Christian teaching about creation.. Later chapters will expound the themes here presented.

The Christian doctrine of creation is not simply an explanation of the origin of the universe. It holds that God is transcendent and free, that the creatures are contingent and free, that the ongoing world of history and events in the world are purposive, that within that human history the purpose of creation is being revealed, that the Redeemer is the Creator. It also teaches that the creation reaches its fulfilment at the end, at the eschaton.

All statements of faith are statements about God and his activity.

Christian statements about God are at the same time statements about Jesus Christ.

The Christian doctrine of creation results from addressing these questions: What is the meaning and significance of Christian faith? How are we to understand that faith? What is entailed in the fellowship with God that constitutes Christian faith?

'God is Creator' is a primary confession of such faith. Without the action of the transcendent, creative God of love and power in Jesus Christ there could be no such thing as Christian faith.

Christian faith in God the Creator is not a cosmology. That is to say, it is not identical with an explanation of the beginning of the physical universe.

What the Christian says about creation is a result of experiencing and reflecting on the experience of salvation. Such experience is seen as an act of creation. Paul remarks, 'If any man is in Christ, he is a new creature' (II *Corinthians*. 5:17). He has experienced the love of God, and continues to experience that love. This is the love of the sovereign God, the God of power, who imparts himself to his creatures, but remains sovereign.

Such creative activity is continuous throughout human history.

The will of God the Creator has been revealed in Christ. Only the transcendent God of power can save. The power of love directed to the creatures and productive of fellowship with the creature is the power of the Creator. Only as it is can there be salvation.

So the Christian insists that this is revealed in Christ. The Son, the 'Word' is none other than the divine. 'God was in Christ'. 'The word was God' 'The word was made flesh.'

The Christian realises that he has come to the very boundaries of his knowledge and understanding when speaking about the creative love of God. Hence he makes his confession in gratitude and humility.

Confession of creation does not consist in a psychological statement about a special kind of human experience, i.e. it is not a creature-centred exposition. That does not mean that such an investigation is not legitimate in its own right. But, like a literalistic understanding of beginnings, it has nothing to do with the unique interest of the believer, which is to speak about God in creative action. The Christian understanding of creation is quite other than scientific.

When we start with the New Testament, we find that the concern is not primarily with the fact and the manner of creation.

The New Testament is concerned with 'the reason why the world was created and to what end.' The story of the creation in *Genesis* says nothing about this. The Prologue to the Gospel of *John* is quite distinct in its approach. Here the creation is mentioned in a way we find nowhere else in the Bible. Here it is clear that when Christian believers speak of the creation, they mean something different from 'explaining' why there is a world or why things exist. Here there is no question of confusing the creation with a cosmogony. The problems addressed are different from those of *Genesis*. Here it is a question of the relation between the present existence of man and man as created by God, the problem of the meaning of the Fall. If there is in the New Testament a question of 'why?' it concerns the purpose, the 'end' of creation.

The love of God is the final cause of creation. The 'ideal reason' for the creation is revealed in Jesus Christ. This is why the Old Testament story of creation cannot be the starting point for the Christian doctrine of creation. Nothing of this is expressed there. For the New Testament, the purpose of the creation is revealed in Jesus Christ who is the Word, the *logos* of the creation. That purpose is that 'in the fullness of times he (God) might gather together in one all things in him both which are in heaven and which are on earth, even in him.' *Ephesians* 1:10. Here there is a similarity of reference with a difference in content from the *Genesis* account. The language there is of the heavens and the earth. The context is transformed. Here it is quite obvious that to raise questions about the relation between science and faith is quite peripheral The same is also true of the earlier creation story in the book of *Genesis*.

Christians understand creation rightly

(1) by starting with the New Testament and with faith in Jesus Christ, by setting all discussion in the context of the New Testament revelation.

(2) by then looking at the complex picture encapsulated in *Genesis* 1-3, and by remembering that the creation is the prelude to the Fall, that our human history is the history of fallen humanity. The product of the creation is a fallen world, a fallen humanity;

(3) by seeing the purpose of the writers of the *Genesis* creation stories in the context both of the history of the Hebrews and in the context of the salvation history that produced Christian faith. This will involve engaging in some serious examination of the literary history of the documents.

1

FAITH AND SCIENCE

A Christian doctrine of creation is of a different order from a scientific explanation of the origin of the universe. Rightly understood, there can be no conflict with such scientific accounts.

It is a mistake to seek support for belief in creation from science. Creationists often wish to have science on their side. So they create their own science. Holding to the 'absolute truth' of the biblical account, and faced with the geological evidence, they find themselves bound to give an alternative explanation of several things, for example, the existence of fossils. One might hear, as I heard recently, 'Fossils did not form over time.' I mention this simply to show that it is misguided to seek support for faith in science. The case just mentioned is an example of the distortion of science in the attempt to support a faith which is thought to require support from science. This is an example of the unsatisfactory method of interpretation of a biblical passage. Other examples are easily found.

The need to appeal to science is a direct deduction from the literalistic approach to the creation narrative of *Genesis*. Creationists must have science on their side since their claim is about the age of the earth and the simultaneous emergence of the universe. So there must be scientific evidence for the fundamentalist claims. The literalist says. 'I require that science be on my side. But scientists say x when I say y. And y contradicts x. So I say that y can be shown to be scientifically correct. So I provide my own scientific account. The reason is that it has to be scientifically correct for my literalistic interpretation of *Genesis* to be correct. So I find an alternative explanation of the age of the earth, involving me in statements about the geology of the fossils etc.'

Did God create dogs? Or only wolves? This is a concrete way
of focussing on the question, 'How from the initial emergence of
the world did we arrive at the present state of the universe?' For it
is quite evident that our world is very different from the biblical
picture. It is an interesting question if we wish to consider how creatures developed within the physical world. So, interesting though
it is, it is a subsidiary, or even a non-essential problem as far as the
Christian doctrine of creation is concerned. Given that there were
wolves, the question of how dogs developed or were developed
from them is not a religious, but obviously a scientific problem.
So we look to the scientist for answers. That is, if we are interested
enough to inquire.

Appropriate language and the open mind

Before engaging in intelligent discussion on any subject, we
must master the vocabulary. That means learning new words.

While engaging in discussion, we will ask the appropriate
questions. It takes patience to be able to recognise the importance
of questions you may not have before considered.

Similarly, you may not always understand what someone is
claiming. Then you are tempted just to pass on. But you may in
that act of bracketing miss something essential. So persist. It may
mean that you have not yet mastered the vocabulary.

We do not start afresh when we come to think about creation.
Those before us who have asked the question, 'Why is there anything?' have left us with a range of words, terms, and arguments.
We acknowledge our debt to them and find our own way with
their help.

The terms we use to discuss the topic are crucial. If we insist
on imposing a strict limit to the terms we are ready to use, we
may find that we are not able to make progress in understanding.
Where language is restricted and ideas are not 'expansible', where
it is insisted that 'You talk my restricted language, otherwise I shall
not listen!' dialogue and progress are not possible.

But since the subject we are here talking about is the transcendent God and the coming to be of everything, the emergence of being itself, we shall be ready to acknowledge the need for appropriate and difficult terms.

So our mind must be open for consideration and appropriation of suitable language. For the language we successfully use to talk about the ordinary things of our lives will not prove adequate to approach the largest and most basic problem of all — the existence of all that is when there might have been nothing. But of course that is the only language we have. So it is the only language we can use. That means we shall have to do something with that language when we use it to talk about creation and about the transcendent God, Maker of Heaven and Earth.

Different kinds of inquiry

Only if one understands the distinction between the kind of questions asked and the kind of inquiries being made by the religious, the philosophical, the historical, and the scientific can one reasonably understand the uniqueness of the theological account of creation. For, since the religious understanding of creation and so the questions it raises are unique, *sui generis*, and so quite distinguishable from other sorts of question only confusion results if the appropriate distinctions are not made.

Where philosophical inquiry impinges on religious interests, we shall have to take note of and to understand its discussions and conclusions. We shall in this writing give consideration, where appropriate, to the questions raised and solutions suggested by such inquiries. These are interesting in themselves, quite apart from the importance they have for our particular concerns.

If scientific methods and scientific conclusions are quite distinguishable from the religious interest, then there are two spheres which do not overlap and science cannot and does not pose a threat to religious affirmations about creation. Nor can the religious approach determine what the scientific problems are and how they should be approached.

Historical and scientific claims

What also is clear is that, while the serious believer and the Christian theologian give attention to historical claims, there is no identity between such historical claims and the unique theological claims the religious person makes. So neither history nor science pose a threat to the claims the religious person makes about creation. The exception is when the proponent of creation insists that we give a literal account of the origin of all things at the initiative of a transcendent God and takes a single biblical passage (*Genesis* 1-3) as providing that account. When the believer insists that that account demands scientific corroboration, i.e. overlaps with scientific accounts of origins, and that he must provide his alternative scientific account, he finds himself threatened when the given scientific accounts differ from his own.

So questions arise. What is the nature of this threat? Is it a threat to his faith? Or to his entrenched belief? Or is the non-religious account irrelevant to that faith, but nevertheless worthy on its own terms? That is a question to be decided on scientific and historical terms, not religious ones. How could a religious conviction lead to scientific conclusions?

The Historical

Also, when the believer insists that the account is to be set in a particular historical frame, to be worked out by interpreting Old Testament accounts of early history so that an actual date for the creation can be inferred, he finds that his historical account of ancient history differs from those of secular historians. So an ignorance of, or an unwillingness to engage in exploring the literary history of the Scripture provides ground for further conflict.

Take the account of beginnings in *Genesis* as literal and historical and then attempt to place it in its context in a literally understood Old Testament account of events, and there then emerges the idea of a recent beginning of the world by working backward from the events within the created order. So we get the idea of a 'young earth'. As with the comment about the scientific, such literalistic engagements have nothing to do with a Christian doctrine of creation.

All that is here accomplished is that a physical universe is placed in a context of historical events, and a chronology for it is given. The literalist's claim is that the account is be set in a particular historical frame. That frame is the Old Testament account of early history. The source is taken as an authentic historical account of the first centuries of human existence. Interpret these sources and an actual date for the creation of the world, the actual point of the 'beginning' can be achieved. The creationist, as he has come to be called, then finds that his historical accounting differs from other historical accounts of ancient history. While he arrives at the date of 4004 B.C. as the date of creation, other historians are giving firm evidence for the existence of established civilisations by that time.

Such discussions are only a side-line, of no relevance for religious claims. Historical conclusions are not religious confessions. Being of a different order of claim, they have no relevance for a Christian doctrine of creation.

The crux of the matter is that God is in relation to the creatures whose history he has made possible. That is what is important. The specification of the time of creation is quite irrelevant when we speak of that redemptive relationship. The one who redeems is the Creator of all. That is what is important. The one who redeems is none other than the omnipotent creator. 'The *logos* was God' *John* 1:1-3.

What sidetracking takes place! What effort we spend in apparent debates about the development of the cosmos and its creatures! What toils we make to argue for or against a recent creative act! How can we be so easily led into replacing witness to the Gospel with barren claims of a pseudo-scientific and pseudo-historical flavour!

Given a clear distinction between theology, history, and science there is no threat. But the crucial question remains, 'How shall limited and contingent beings use language employed within that contingent and limited existence of one God, who transcends that limitation? i.e. How shall creatures speak of the Creator?'

2

Two different questions and alternative understandings

For the sake of clarity, let us distinguish the two questions:
(1) What constitutes a Christian doctrine of creation?
(2) What is the explanation of the origin of the physical world?

Since the present state of the world is related to its origin, the question 'What is the relation between the origin and present condition of the cosmos?' is inevitable and will immediately follow.

Acknowledging that there are alternative understandings of these questions or even of their respective status, what results if one is confused with the other? It may even be the case that one replaces the other or that two sets of beliefs are held in two compartments of the mind (as it were). One obvious result is that one just has no interest in the alternative understanding. One kind of understanding is taken as prime and exclusive. One reason given may be that they are considered to be incompatible. Another is that the status given to one excludes due consideration of the other.

Many Christians of course hold firm and sincere beliefs about salvation and are prepared to maintain these beliefs, often at great cost to themselves. But unfortunately, even given so much in the Scriptural writings to guide them, they frequently isolate their discussion of creation from such beliefs.

Our concern is with the Christian account of creation. The concern to give an account problem of the origin of the universe is a different problem. Of course, one will also be aware of explanations of origins. But here are two kinds of questions and explanations.

Since they are of different kinds, their function and their status are different. One can follow each satisfactorily, provided they are not confused.

Our concern is that to focus exclusively on origins of the physical world leads to neglect of, and failure of, interest in the more important question, 'What is the Christian doctrine of creation, of God as Creator, of the Word as creative, of the ongoing course of history?' Exclusive attention to the opening words of *Genesis* and to the question of the origin of the universe as a literal occurrence is only peripheral to a Christian understanding of creation.

The two approaches are quite distinct. So the answers to these two different questions will be quite different.

Christians are theists. So the account Christians give of creation will be a theistic one. It will expound creation in terms of the activity of God, the Creator. These essential features of a theistic doctrine will feature in the development of a distinctive Christian doctrine. What follows is an example of an acceptable theistic doctrine of creation.

1. there is other reality than God and that is really other than he.
2. there is other reality than God because God speaks.
3. God commands the world to be, this command is obeyed, and the event of obedience is the existence of the world.
4. all the preceding holds in the present tense.
5. the creature simply in that it is a creature has an absolute beginning. The *Genesis* story is not a myth for it does not tell us what things were like when there were no things.
6. reality other than God not only has a beginning but also has an end in that it has a goal.
7. the world God creates is not a thing, a 'cosmos', but rather a history. God creates a history that is a world.
8. the biblical doctrine of creation is centrally a doctrine of the creation of life.[1]

---

1   Robert W. Jenson expounds these statements in *Systematic Theology Volume 2 The Works of God*. Oxford: University Press, 1999. pp. 5-16.

When the object of discussion is world or universe, the questions are

Q1   How did the universe come to be?

Q2   How shall we understand the Creator, God revealed in Jesus Christ as related to the existence, still continuing, of the world of objects and persons?

Focussing on Q1 may well lead to neglect, to limiting interest, to the making subsidiary of Q2.

The term 'creationist' has become current for the position that focuses exclusively on the physical universe, the interpretation of *Genesis* 1 literally and the position that the earth is of relatively recent origin, roughly six thousand years old. The creationist's understanding of the *Genesis* story as a literal account of the coming into being of the world results from his insistence on the status of Scripture as the inspired and authoritative word of God, to be interpreted literally, without reference to its cultural setting.

Such a reductionist view of the biblical account becomes questionable when attention is exclusively focused on answering Q1. It leads to the claim that what is of primary importance is to produce a literal account of the coming into being of the world and that is all that there is to be said under the rubric of 'creation.' The doctrine of creation is limited to the explanation or assertion of the physical origin of the universe.

But there is nothing religious about that. The biblical account of origins taken as a literal account is then placed directly in relation to any scientific account that proposes to investigate origins. It is also placed in relation to an historical explanation of the literature containing the account. The concern is with the same entity, the universe, and its origin. So we have two sets of explanation in a relation of confrontation, even opposition: literalistic versus scientific and historical and literalistic versus theological. The accounts are in opposition unless there is some way of harmonising them

Such a literal understanding of the statement concerning the origin of the cosmos cannot feature in a *theology* of creation. The reason is that the literalistic interpretation is made in isolation from the religious faith of the believer. Therefore, to assert the coming into being of a developed universe in six days is simply irrelevant to a theological understanding of creation. Moreover, it is 'untrue scientifically' and philosophically and 'religiously irrelevant'.

> 'If the idea of creation represents . . . a literal and objective truth about the origin of the world, a homely description about the originating process of the world system, then it has no religious character. Such a description may point to an interesting fact which satisfies our inquiries about the first days of the world, but it has no relevance to our lives beyond that flash of momentary curiosity. As an objective truth about the world's beginning it has no deep reverberating bearing on our own existence and destiny; it is not truth about which all men are ultimately concerned.'[2]

Cosmology and revelation

Once there was no world. We live in a 'world'. Given that world, there are laws that explain the transition from non-being to being, the being in which we now participate, and the history of which we can trace. But we can ask the question of origins. In doing so, we then at the limits of our understanding.

> The 'Maker of heaven and earth' is not the beginning. The Beginning is merely the limit at which man arrives when he asks, "Whence?" The kerygma (= the earliest preaching of the Gospel) does not dispel all mysteries connected with the transition from non-being to being. We might even say it dispels none of them. What it does say is that the Whence, that from which we have our existence, is none other than the one

---

2   Langdon Gilkey, *Maker of Heaven and Earth*. New York: Doubleday and Company, Inc. 1959. p. 285.

from whom we have forgiveness. Not only redemption but existence itself is given to us. Existence is an act of grace. This is what we mean by God as Creator, namely, the one who in grace enabled being to be. The phrase "In the beginning God created". . . . is not a cosmological but a revelational assertion. It does not mean, "Our calculations show that the Beginning is God." Rather, it means, "The Word that was made flesh came not into an alien world but into his own world." In other words the power of the God who redeems the world extends over the world."[3]

The inheritance: The cyclical view of the Greeks

Philosophers discussed the universe and provided ideas for further consideration, which were influential for centuries and helped to shape theological explanation.

The Greeks believed in eternity, an eternity manifested in the ever recurring of events in the experienced world. They were fascinated by the idea of form. To understand this, we must grasp the Greek urgency to be constantly striving for perfection of form. They strove to produce that perfection of form, both in art and in the human body. They employed the idea of perfection of form in their explanation of the cosmos. They had clear and distinct ideas about that.

Perfection of form manifests itself in the circle. They were aware of and fascinated by the constant change that was taking place in every sphere of experience. They spoke of change and motion as synonymous. So perfect motion is cyclical. They observed the night skies and charted the movements of the planets and, in doing so, applied these ideas of form and perfection to what they observed. In the orderly universe, planets moved in circular orbits.

---

3   Edward Farley, *The Transcendence of God*. London: Epworth Press, 1962, p. 204.

They applied this belief to the events within the cosmos. Here events manifested order, an order that consisted in the recurring of objects and communities within the cosmos. Perfection was manifest in endless recurrence, endless cycles. For them there was no absolute creator. So there was no beginning to nature and history. Movement and change are eternal. Events repeat themselves in an everlasting cycle. In doing so, 'time both mirrors the static perfection of eternity and illustrates the immanent harmony of all nature.'[4]

Plato (429-347 B. C.) gave an account of beginnings The demiurge produced the cosmos. The Greek term *demiourgos*, transliterates into 'demiurge' in English. It is a combination of two roots, *demos* meaning 'public' and *ergon* meaning 'work'. Literally it means 'someone who works for the people.' The Greeks used it of the magistrate. It is also used for a workman, a handicraftsman and generally for a maker or author.[5]

In Plato, it is a name for the maker of the world. It was also used later by the Gnostics, but for them the *demiourgos* was subordinate to the Supreme Being.

Plato's theory of the universe is a theory about how it came to be. He expounds his theory in his dialogue *Timaeus*. (References in the text are to sections in this work.)

Plato is interested in the relation between the unchangeable and the changeable. He produces a cosmology (= a theory of the totality of phenomena in space and time) and a cosmogony (= a theory of the generation of the universe). So, recognising the distinction between describing what is in being, the structure of the universe, and giving an account of its formation, of how it came to be, Plato presents cosmology (an account of what is) in relation to the cosmogony (an account of how it came to be) .

There is an ideal world, eternal, perfect, and unchanging. This is the realm of Forms, of Ideas. The *demiourgos*, the world maker, is good, a beneficent creator, but 'past finding out' (28). He desires to

---

4   Langdon Gilkey, *op cit.*, p. 245
5   Liddell and Scott, *Lexicon*, Oxford: Clarendon Press, 1958.

communicate his goodness, his perfection, to creatures other than himself. 'God desired that all things should be good and nothing bad, so far as this was attainable' (30). He fashioned the world of sense, a constantly changing world, on the model of the eternal world of the unchanging Ideas. 'The world was made in a perfect form, that of a globe, sphere' (33).

Thus, he argues, the physical universe is a unity not a plurality. It is a unity comprised of soul and body, created not out of nothing but of formerly existing proportions and elements: 'The soul . . . began a divine beginning of never-ceasing and rational life enduring throughout all time' (36, 37). The soul of the world is the origin of all movement.

Time, regular measured duration, begins with the coming into being of the ordered universe: 'He resolved to have a moving image of eternity . . . he made this image eternal but moving according to number, while eternity itself rests in unity; and this image we call time . . . .Time and the heaven came into being at the same instant' (37). In the universe there is constant change. Before the world came to be, there was no change. So there was nothing for time to measure. With the emergence of the changeable universe, time was introduced with change. Without change, time is meaningless. 'Motion', 'moving', is a synonym for change.

Plato insists that our knowledge of such things is limited and we must just do the best we can. As mortal we must accept our limitations. 'we must remember that I who am speaker and you who are the judges are only mortal men. And we ought to accept the tale which is probable and inquire no further' (28). Excellent advice as we continue!

Aristotle (384-322 B.C.) observed constant change and decay in the world of our experience. His observations of such mutability provide him with a problem. He questioned, 'Why are there such finite existences? Why does the existence of finite phenomena not terminate in nothing? Why does the perishable and changeable continue in existence, constantly repeating itself in an endless cycle? In his exposition, *Aristotle* provides an extensive analysis of change.

He argued that the continuing existence of the heavenly bodies with their circular motions and the unceasing courses of the ephemeral duration of the phenomena of our world of experience require explanation. So he proceeded to give one. Movement demands a mover. Contingent movement and change demands an absolute, beyond movement and change. There is an absolute ground of the change and temporal in the unchanging and eternal.

But Plato's eternal forms cannot provide the explanation. For there must be an agent, an active principle, an eternal principle whose essence is actuality. This is the Unmoved Mover. which causes perfect movement while itself unmoved. Such perfect movement is movement in space, and perfection is movement in a circle:

> '. . . . this the first mover causes and cannot be
> subject to. There is, then, something which is always
> moved with an unceasing motion, which is motion in
> a circle, and this is plain not in theory only, but in fact.
> Therefore the first heaven must be eternal.'[6]

Thomas Aquinas (A.D. 1225-1274), the great systematic theologian of the Middle Ages, was so often dependent upon *Aristotle*. Nevertheless, he took issue with him here. God's transcendence of the created world involves his existence in eternity. It also involves that the world has its source in his will. The world is therefore not eternal. He wrote:

> God is prior to the world by priority of duration.
> But the word *prior* signifies priority, not of time, but
> of eternity. . . . from the eternal action of God an
> eternal effect does not follow; there follows only such
> an effect as God has willed, an effect, namely which
> has being after non-being.'[7]

---

6   Aristotle, *Metaphysics*. 1072a 20, 26. Mc Keon edition, p. 879

7   *Summa Theologica* Q. 46 Art.1 Reply objections 8, 10

These two claims of Thomas form the basis of any acceptable theistic doctrine of creation. But we must remind ourselves that a theistic doctrine of creation is not, or not yet, a Christian doctrine of creation.

God is transcendent. His being is 'from himself', *a se*.

In contrast, created beings are dependent. Their being is derived.

3

ANALOGY

When we speak of God, we use what language we have. This is drawn from our relations with other human beings and from our experience of nature. We can express well our understanding of human relations in the language we inherit and create for that purpose. Our language is thus anthropomorphic, i.e. derived from and expressive of what we know of persons. We often use such language of impersonal things. We very often apply the terms we use of the human (*anthropos* = man= the human) to the non-human where they do not literally apply, but where they are nevertheless expressive of meaning. We apply our personal language to all levels of being, lower as well as higher. We speak of cruel storms (when they cause damage). of sympathetic dogs (when they act in a 'friendly' way) of stupid machines (when they go wrong). We also ascribe human features, attributes and forms, to higher levels of being. God is angry, loving, generous. It is especially when we do this that our question arises. If we apply human features to the transcendent deity, do we not talk beyond our understanding and so end up with paradoxes we cannot resolve? If we cannot avoid doing so, we may have to accommodate ourselves to the fact that we must live with paradox.

So the question arises: Does the way of analogy rely upon paradoxical anthropomorphisms?

It is appropriate to point out that this problem is not only for the thinker, but also for the theologian. We are constantly using analogy in our ordinary talk. The believer is not alone. But we must focus on the believer. So we can for example ask the question: What does it mean for the sincere believer in his devotions to say, or sing?

'I come to the garden alone
While the dew is still on the roses and
He walks with me and he talks with me
And he tells me I am his own.'?

Such anthropomorphic language is found everywhere in the Scriptures. The Creator walks in the garden, and searching for Adam calls out the question, 'Where are you?' God converses with Abraham, with Job, with Jeremiah. He addresses Saul on the Damascus road.

How can we thus speak of the transcendent God in personal terms? Surely these terms are properly confined to finite beings and relations and are only applicable to our own limited human relations? How can they be used meaningfully of God as the source of all? How can we talk of God as Creator, 'Maker of heaven and earth' in the language of human action and human history?

An influential theological tradition attempts to answer this question by claiming to prove that God exists. What results is an impersonal conception of God, not the transcendent Creator of all existence. Even if the proof were satisfactory, the believer would not recognise the result as the Creator God of living faith.

In employing analogy, we move from what we know, what we have experienced or observed, to what we do not know, but would like to know. We start with where we are, and project to where we would like to be. We look for some likeness where there is mostly difference.

We know a lot about the natural world. We know a lot about the world of human experience. Does what we know tell us anything about what is beyond the world we know, about the creator or even about the process of creation? Does it enable us to say that we have good reason to believe in creation and an intelligent creator? Some believers are quite certain that we can use analogy to answer these questions. We may project to a relationship with which we are not familiar, from one with which we are.

The relationship of cause and effect, of one thing related to another in cause-effect fashion with which we are familiar, is based on the distinction between the object made and the maker of the object. This is based on our experience of the familiar, the experience of associating the thing made to the maker of the thing. We then project that association to the relationship with which we are not familiar. We move from the existence of World which we interpret as World created to Creator. With the help of this analogy, it is proposed that we can move beyond our familiar knowledge of world to knowledge of a transcendent and intelligent Creator. The analogy is between the relation of the maker of something to the thing made, the relation of cause and effect, to the relation of Cosmos created to Creator. God making the cosmos is analogous to the craftsman making the product. The move is a simple one, and can be stated very simply.

The world shows evidence of order.

Order involves design.

There is no design without a designer.

Therefore the world has a designer.

That designer is God, the Creator.

The argument can be elaborated and become very sophisticated.

Think about a machine that most of us carry around with us constantly. I am not a watchmaker and have never made the opportunity to observe a watchmaker at work, nor to learn how a watch is constructed. But I have no doubt, indeed I know, that watches are made by watchmakers. I know that there is a process of construction resulting in a fully operative watch.

An argument was very popular in the eighteenth century elaborated and classically stated by William Paley (1743-1805), in his book, *Natural Theology*.

He constructed an analogy between the workings of a watch and the workings of nature. We can certainly find order in the cosmos. We take such order for granted. We can find more and more, if we are careful to look: for example the clockwork functioning of the heavenly bodies, enabling astronomers to predict with uncanny accuracy such phenomena as eclipses, centuries before they occur. If the watch and nature are similar in their operations, we can then move from the observed to the unobserved. We begin by moving from the watch to the watchmaker, and thence from the 'works of nature' with its undoubted order to the intelligent designer, to a Creator.

The problem is that we have not moved from the phenomena within the world to a reality independent of the world. The 'unmoved mover' of Aquinas and the world-maker of Paley do not transcend the cosmos. Both the watch and the watchmaker are phenomena within the cosmos. There is no question here of moving beyond. Originally there was no natural structure. After creation there was. So the analogy fails at this crucial point.

The final step in the classical statement of the arguments from cause, motion, and design made by Aquinas is to identify the First Cause, the Unmoved Mover, the Designer with God. He concludes his argument with a grand leap to the conclusion:

> 'Therefore it is necessary to arrive at a first mover, moved by no other; and this everyone understands to be God.'[8]

What is meant by 'necessary to arrive' is that it is logically necessary, that we are compelled by logical necessity to deduce the identity. But he gives no such justification for taking the bold step of identifying the First Mover with God the Creator. He simply says that everybody does this.

But to identify the Unmoved Mover with God, to move from within the system to a Creator outside of the ordered system is to go beyond the logic of the argument. We have moved from philosophical argument to confession of faith. We have moved from within the system to beyond the system, from the immanent to the transcendent.

---

8   *Summa Theologica*, Question 2 Article 3.

The procedure here is simple. We find an analogy between two different entities in their intricacy and order and speak of design. We then take the further, crucial step from the world of nature to a Designer. We take account of the vast difference between a simple watch and the intricate world of nature and speak of the difference between their source. The watchmaker is human. The Creator is transcendent.

Thomas Aquinas claims that we know *that* he is from the argument. *What* he is and the process of his relationship to the world is still beyond us. In this way, he thinks to preserve the transcendence of the Creator. We cannot know *what* God is. We cannot say what attributes he has unless he in some way reveals himself to us. So he moves from philosophical argument to appeal to revelation.

Often the argument is stated extremely simply. Doesn't the beauty, the harmony, the regularity of nature show that there is a Creator and Sustainer? It appears in different forms, often in the popular religious press accompanied by splendid pictures of the beauties of the natural world. Unfortunately, it has not lost its appeal as an argument.

> 'To prove God by philosophy is neither good philosophy nor good theology, and of no real help either to unbeliever or to believer. To the first, God is never actually proved; to the second, a proved God is never satisfactory — and both are right.'[9]

The creation model makes the development of science possible

The Christian doctrine of creation enables us to see the world in a particular way, in a way quite different from metaphysics or science. But the emergence of science owes its origin to the very viewpoint that it later rejects. That viewpoint provides us with a vision of the cosmos. That vision sees the universe as orderly, not

---

9   Gilkey, *op. cit.*, p. 266.

under the control of irrational or malignant forces. It provides us
with a model in terms of which we can think about the universe
and the context in which we live. It not only encouraged a special
sort of religious practice but, as time passed, it provided for the beginnings of scientific investigation The demons and gods had to be
exorcised before there could emerge an understanding of the world
as orderly and predictable and so capable of precise and accurate
description and determination. For if the cosmos and human life
is at the mercy of evil and unmanageable forces, there could be no
possibility for human security, nor for reasonable understanding.

There is something of an irony in the ensuing development.
Initially, with Newton and other early scientists, there appeared no
conflict with Christian beliefs. But, as science progressed and the
empirical method became firmly established in scientific practice
and stoutly defended by empirical philosophers, that very scientific
progress led to rationalism and secularism. That meant that the
cosmos could be and was analysed by means of scientific methods
that had no need for the concept of a Creator. One remembers the
reply made to Napoleon when he asked the scientist 'What about
the Creator?' 'I have no need of that hypothesis!' was the answer
he received from Laplace that expressed what became a very widely
accepted viewpoint. Secularism has its roots in developments from
the Christian doctrine of creation.

Literal and non-literal language

The assertion 'God is Creator' poses sharply the basic question,
How shall we meaningfully speak of God? One pronounces that
sentence believing that it has content and is making a claim and
that the claim is true. Another hears the claim and replies that it
is meaningless. The questions then arise, What does the statement
'God is Creator' mean? Assuming that it has meaning, how may
one show that it is a true statement?

The alternatives are that it is either meaningless or false.

So we must pursue the quest for the meaning of the claim
about God. This leads us to the distinction between how, if it is

making a claim, the claim is to be taken. For there are different kinds of truth. The distinction between literal and metaphorical meaning arises when we are presented with different versions of the idea that God is Creator.

The fundamentalist claims that 'God is Creator', 'Maker of heaven and earth' is to be taken quite literally. The act of creation can be spoken of and understood as we use our ordinary language and be taken with the ordinary meanings we give to the language we are using. A potter makes a pot. A housewife makes a cake. An inventor conceives the device and then produces a bouncing bomb. So God, the acting subject, makes a physical and personal world. There is a series of temporal events as the production progresses until the physical and personal universe emerges into reality and is complete. This understanding, reliant as it is upon the first words of the Bible in the book of *Genesis*, defines creation as the bringing into being of a previously non-existing world. And there the interest rests.

Asked for the grounds for the belief, the fundamentalist asserts that the Bible is authoritative. Its words, i.e. its propositions, are literally true. No further warrant is required. No further rationale is needed. There is no place for a contrary view. There can be no question of further defence. One rests the case for a six day creation on the authority of Scripture interpreted as literally authoritative. There can be no further debate if that view of Scripture is maintained.

The Story Form

In *Genesis,* creation is presented in the form of a story. Indeed there are two versions of that story.

In the first story (*Genesis* 1) God remains above, transcendent. There is no struggle against opposing gods or evil beings or other forces. The story as told by the Hebrew sets forth the Creator as alone, sublime. It is quite and utterly unique among the creation stories of the ancient world. In those myths the world comes to be

as the result of conflict between rival gods. Such mythical elements
in the other Eastern creation stories are absent here.

The form of expression of the *Genesis* stories is that of narrative
symbol, of story. So pause a little with the idea of 'story'. Details
within stories do not have to be consistent if their purpose is not
to narrate exactly what happened, but to point to meanings. So
with these stories. It does not take a day for God to say 'Let there
be light', nor for the light to appear, 'and there was light'. Here
immediate creation takes place with the utterance of the word. We
are in the context of a story. Our question must be to ask what the
story means. What does it tell us about God?

One narrative says 'He created them male and female' The
other says that God took of the dirt of the ground and formed a
male being and breathed into his nostrils the 'breath' of life. Then,
having created the male, further activity was required. So God op-
erated upon the man, making a human female out of a male rib.
The very physical nature of these actions invites us to ask simple
questions. But we remember that the literary form is that of a story.
The Hebrew presents meaning and truth in the form of a story. This
is in contrast to the Greeks, where truth is presented in the form of
a system, exemplified supremely and superbly in *Aristotle*.

The fact is that to insist that language about the transcendent
is literally true is to divest it of all religious or spiritual relevance. So
'The world was created in six days' is taken as a true statement of an
objective fact about the bringing into being of a physical universe.
Why is that statement to be taken as having such significance for
faith any more than any other statement about objective facts or
events within the universe? Such statements of physical facts about
and within the universe, in this case about their origin, simply have
no relevance of a religious kind. Such a statement is like any other
concerning what happens within the physical universe.

At the same time, the conviction of classical theism that God
is transcendent is also as firmly held by the conservative Christian.
Again there can be no denial of the very clear passages of Scripture
which forcefully assert this. How then shall we speak literally of

what is transcendent to our knowledge and so to our language? The fact is that we cannot do so.

Since God the Creator is transcendent, language about him must be appropriately qualified to have meaning for creatures who exist within the limited finite world which he in his eternity has created. God is 'other' than the creature. So our language, which has been formed and is appropriate for use in speaking of relations within our finite and limited world, may not be at all appropriate to speak of the transcendent Creator. So we have to consider whether due qualification may be made of that human language so that it may be meaningfully employed in speaking of God. If so, we shall ask what sort of qualification it is appropriate to make to our ordinary language. If not, we shall not speak of God. God becomes ineffable. If we consider that no human language is at all suitable, we shall be silent.

Theologians and philosophers long ago asked the question: Does God have attributes? This question may be explained by providing further questions. Is God free? Is God powerful? Is God loving? Is God good? The attributes here are freedom, power, love, goodness. Is it possible and proper to attribute such qualities to the transcendent God for he is other than we. He is not bound by the limits we experience. What might it mean to attribute such attributes to God since we cannot go beyond the boundaries fixed to our knowledge by the limitations of our experience? We are creatures. He is Creator.

Two answers are given. Some say 'Yes!, we can make affirmations of such attributes.' Others say 'No! We can only make denials.'

Those who said 'yes' have difficult tasks on their hands, or rather for their minds! What shall we do with our ordinary words when we wish to use them meaningfully of the God who is 'other' than we? The answers given were varied: to employ the *way of analogy* and the *way of eminence* the *via analogiae,* and the *via eminentiae.* Those who say 'No' developed the *way of negation,* the *via negativa.*

Each of the alternatives is an example of how non-literal language has been used in relation to God.

The *way of analogy* proceeds by taking a feature from our human experience and qualifying it by retaining a point of connection, namely a similarity between what is taken as a basis of comparison, while at the same time specifying a point or points of difference.

The *way of eminence* takes an attribute found in human beings and qualifies it by saying that it is present 'to an eminent degree' in the one to whom it is attributed. So God's freedom is unlike ours in that, as his attribute, it is defined as being in the highest degree possible. But that is still not to transcend the human. For we can conceive something greater than the greatest degree of human perfection. But God is 'that than which no greater can be conceived.'

The *way of negation* simply denies that features found in the human are to be employed of the transcendent. What results is that God is not spatial, not bound by the limits of time, not mortal, etc. The more we deny of God the less he becomes, until denying all, he becomes a figure (?) of complete negation.

We are now ready to consider some classical discussions.

creatio ex nihilo

The formula *creatio ex nihilo* provides one example of language qualified for theological use. It says that the origin of the creation is in God alone. Nothing existed 'before' creation. but God and his Word.

First, it says that *creatio*, i.e. the word 'creation, is not to be taken in its normal sense when we use it of bringing something into being by using pre-existing materials. The housewife has her ingredients. The potter has her clay. The inventor has all kinds of things to hand. Of the transcendent Creator we must use the term in a different and unique way. We must provide it with an unusual sense. Creation is in our experience and so in our way of speaking not 'out of nothing'. To add that qualifier means that we are taking our experience of creating and using it as an analogy to make a unique claim. Talk about God must be duly qualified talk.

It is clear that we do not have experience of this kind of creating. So by analogy we are predicating of the Creator an activity of which we have had no experience. We might imagine such activity, but we have not experienced it. Moreover, we are transferring the idea of creating to a being beyond our limited resources. What guarantee do we have, indeed could we have, that it is appropriate? What is transcendent is beyond us, beyond our knowledge and experience. We have reached the limits of our knowledge.

Second, the use of this formula was employed in the church to deny certain heretical views which emerged in her early history. This finds expression in a statement of a leading nineteenth century theologian.

> 'The origin of the world must be traced entirely to the divine activity, but not in such a way that this activity is thought of as resembling human activity; and the origin of the world must be presented as the event in time which conditions all change, but not as to make the divine activity itself a temporal activity. If we speak of the pre-existence of form before things we shall say they exist in God and not outside God.'[10]

This position contrasts to those that construe the process of creation as in the one hand like

(1) human methods of construction which give form to an already existing matter, or on the other hand like

(2) the processes of nature in the composition of bodies out of many elements.

(1) For examples, take the process of making a fence or producing an automobile. The materials ('matter') are first collected and shaped. Then they are put together as the product begins to take shape, when 'form' is imposed on the matter.

(2) For example, take the growth of a plant. We sow the seed. We provide appropriate conditions. It gathers nourishment at first

---

10 Friedrich Schleiermacher, *The Christian Faith*. Paragraph 41

from the soil. Later it depends on elements in the atmosphere, light, heat and water. Eventually it produces its own seed and the cycle continues. Nature produces by bringing together a whole lot of elements.

What our author is saying is that it is not satisfactory or even illuminating to try to go beyond the creative act and explain how it took place by analogy from either of these processes. The act of creation is unique and beyond the range of any such analogical explanation.

One of the early heretical views was pantheism. It claimed that whatever exists is identical with God. God and the world are 'one'. God is the 'all'. World is not other than God. Christians denied this. The formula *creatio ex nihilo* was directed against the view that God is identical with reality in its totality. To say that would mean that God's transcendence is denied. Hence no room is left for reality other than God. If reality is emanation from God, and so identical with God, no space is left for an act of creation, for a reality other than God.

The formula 'creation out of nothing' says: Creatures are not made out of the substance of God. Creaturely existence is not one with the existence of God. The creation results 'not from God but out of nothing (*non de deo, sed ex nihilo*)'. There is reality other than God. Before that other reality, the cosmos, there was only God.

The Gnostics had taught that alongside God there was form-less matter out of which God brought the creation into being. This he accomplished by imposing form upon the matter. The formula denies that. It also denies that other beings than God were involved in the creation. It denies a demiurge. There is no subsidiary creator.

As the church made denials of such positions as they emerged, her doctrine of creation became clearer as one after another assertion was articulated. The church in developing her theology owed a debt to those they considered heretical. They prompted her to make articulate and so make clearer the teaching she was defending.

The question arises whether the Hebrews had arrived at such a conception. The phrase itself occurs in a negative form *ouk ex onton* 'not out of what is' in a later Hebrew document (2 *Maccabees* 7:28).

Genesis raises a doubt. It speaks of waters over which the 'spirit' (wind) of God has to move. Chaos had featured in other accounts of creation. Chaos was opposed to the Creator and hindered creation. It had to be overcome before the creation could take place. So a struggle took place as chaos was subdued.

One Old Testament scholar (among others) acknowledges that in the *Genesis* account, there is formless matter as God speaks the word of creation.

> 'Israel did not succeed in surmounting the difficulty of the concept of chaos. This is evident from the words of *Genesis* 1: 'the earth was without form and void and darkness was upon the face of the deep. And the Spirit of God moved upon the face of the waters.' But the Hebrew did not attribute divine power to chaos. Other Oriental versions of creation had given to chaos power opposed to the deity. 'Israel saw chaos as mere material existence before the creation.' We await the New Testament, and certain later apocryphal books to find that the creation is considered 'entirely as God's work and the last remnant of primordial existence [is] abandoned.'[11]

The idea of 'creation out of nothing', if considered to be appropriately applied to the story which *Genesis* tells, nevertheless is a later development. Its intention is to assert the transcendence of the Creator.

It cannot be our task here to examine in detail whether that term is a biblical concept. Numerous biblical passages in both Testaments are suggestive of the idea. But we need not set the idea of 'biblical concept' in contrast to 'theological invention'. The concept

11 Th.C. Vriezen, *Old Testament Theology*, p.21.

emerged and underwent development in the early centuries of the church in its opposition to the various teachings it considered heretical, such as the Gnostic idea that matter was evil, produced by an evil deity. It is a logical step, which the church took, to move from the conviction that in the creation God created matter, to the conclusion that God in his sovereignty created the whole, including matter. So God created 'out of nothing'.

What is clear is that there is plentiful biblical support of the concept of *creatio ex nihilo*. For example: *Isaiah* 40:21, *Proverbs* 8:22-26, *Psalm* 33:6,9, *Isaiah* 44:6,12,24, 45:18, 46:9, *John* 1:3, *Romans* 4:17, *Hebrews* 11:3.

Our task here has been to indicate that the formula has an important place in clarifying the Christian theistic account of the creation.[12]

Creation and Time

We sometimes seem to discover that life repeats itself, that some incidents from our past recur. We sometimes muse: 'Haven't I been here before?' 'Haven't I met you before?' And when the history teacher says. 'History may repeat itself but good historians must not!' he is thinking of repetition on a much larger scale. We can distinguish several levels of this idea: repetition within an individual life; repetition of the whole life; repetition of some events in the historical course, and repetition of the whole course of history on an enormous historical scale.

Suppose that time is infinite and the course of history repeats itself not once, but over and over again without an end. For as there was no beginning there is also no end. This came to be called

12 For further detailed discussion cf. Gerhard May, *Creatio ex nihilo: The Doctrine of 'Creation out of Nothing' in Early Christian Thought.* Edinburgh: T & T Clark, 1994 and Paul Copan, *Is Creatio Ex Nihilo A Post Biblical Invention.* Trinity Journal 17.1 (Spring 1996: 77-93.

the 'myth of the eternal return.' It is a story about the cosmos and events within the cosmos, and has been believed in different forms by many civilisations.

The rational Greeks provided an interesting argument for eternal recurrence. They were most interested in form and order and thought of the cosmos as exemplifying order on the largest possible scale. For them the most perfect of all forms was the circle. They also believed that time is infinite. Putting these assumptions together, they reasoned as follows.

> The divine is changeless. The cosmos is the realm of order and harmony. Change constantly takes place within the cosmos. To approximate to the divine changelessness, the change within the cosmos is circular, the circle being the perfect form. So emerged the widely held idea in the ancient world that things recur in endless cycles, the myth of the 'eternal return.'

Sometimes the question is posed, if God created at some point in time, why did he not create at another point in time, say, much earlier? But is this a meaningful question? It seems to help us to raise the more important, basic question, 'How are we to conceive of time? To say that something exists in time suggests that time has some objective existence and that events occur in the already existing reality. Time, so to speak, stretches out and becomes a kind of abstract receptacle for whatever occurs. It is a receptacle waiting to be filled with events. If that were so, time would have an independent existence. Creation would have taken place in time. Theists deny this.

Here we meet with a clear statement from the theist. God does not create in time. God created time. Since God created time, time is not eternal. So there can be no thought of eternal recurrence. Moreover God reveals himself in events that occur in time. So both the Hebrew and the Christian understandings of creation, and of revelation, open the way to the assertion that history is linear, not cyclical, that some events within that history are to be seem as revealing God's will and indicating a purpose and a goal to human history. In doing so they point to an end, a fulfilment. So beginning is linked to end. A doctrine of creation is also quite definitely an eschatological doctrine.

4

TWO WORDS: 'BEGINNING' AND 'WORD'

We turn our attention to two words that recur in biblical statements about creation. They are found in the opening of *Genesis* and also in the preface to the gospel of *John*. These words, *beginning* and *word*, are of course part of our everyday discourse. For the Hebrew and the Christian, they receive particular significance.

Each of these words, like many others used in biblical and religious contexts, has its particular background. Both have overtones and meanings that you could never discover without becoming aware of those backgrounds. That means that without some knowledge of how they have been used in other contexts than your own, indeed in other contexts than Christian ones, you will fail to grasp their richness. Acquaintance with these is essential for a satisfactory understanding of the idea of creation.

We have an excellent illustration of this in the gospel of *John*. The opening verses of that writing appear enigmatic and puzzling. It is as if, when we approach the passage with our limited acquaintance from our own knowledge of the meaning of the term 'word,' the writer is beyond our comprehension. For 'word' in our language means a sound spoken or a set of letters written. So we pass over the passage and judge it to be mysterious. That is until we examine the range of meanings the term has in the context of the Hebrews and the Greeks.

The statement that opens the Gospel of *John*, starts with the same words (in translation) that open the book of *Genesis*, namely, 'In the beginning . . . .' But John also used another term current among the Greek thinkers, the term *logos*, *word*. By using this term he is placing the idea of creation in a context different from the

Hebrew one, while himself being quite aware of that Hebrew context. In doing so he is giving it a richness of meaning not found in the Old Testament and not elsewhere in the New Testament. He is interpreting the meaning of creation both in relation to the figure of Jesus, in relation to the universe and in relation to God, its 'Maker'. Consider that context.

(1) The Gospel of *John* comes after the life and influence of Jesus, after the coming into being of Christian faith, and after the writing of other Gospels. That means that as he used the term 'word' *logos*, he is giving it a fresh context and so a new meaning. Indeed the *logos* is identified with Jesus. 'The *logos* became flesh.'

(2) *John* comes after Greek thinking and culture, where the term *logos* had a wide interesting and important currency. To understand that will enable us to see what interesting and far-reaching claim the Gospel is making about creation.

(3) In the long course of Jewish history God has spoken to his people in many different ways. What was characteristic was both the voice and the writings of the prophets. The prophetic message was a very influential power in the course of that history. God 'spoke' and the prophet heard and conveyed the 'word of the Lord'. God was the source. The prophet was the intermediary. 'Word' was both the message 'spoken' to the prophet by God, and so the message he 'heard'. It was also the message he himself spoke as he delivered that message or as he attempted to do so. It was what the people heard, or could have heard had they responded appropriately. The word demanded a response. The term was also used of the later, written expression of that message. The Hebrew community was to receive and respond to the 'word'. It was addressed to the whole community, king and subjects. That the word was from God meant that the position of the prophet, whose task was to receive and to deliver it, was often more important than that of the ruler.

The Word 'logos' in Greek thought

We shall now look at the wide and deep significance the Greek thinkers gave to the term *logos*.

When we arrive at knowledge and understanding, we engage in a process of reasoning. As we reason we use language, engage in discourse, speak and manipulate words. Much of our reasoning is about the world in which we live, about the universe. The world has structure. When we employ our reason aright we can explore and understand that structure. When we can express clearly what we understand, we are one with the structure of the world. The Greek term for 'word,' *logos*, expresses the world's intelligibility. The world is rational. The world is permeated by *logos*. Through 'word', *logos*, we come to know and to express our knowledge of that rationally structured world. In a sense, we understand and share its rationality. Since the world is intelligible, we can make intelligible statements, and construct intelligible arguments about it. The intelligibility of the world is matched by the possibility of our understanding it. The rationality of the cosmos is the condition for our understanding it. That rationality comes from our understanding of it. Understanding, rational thinking, are the products of *logos*. So the rationality of the cosmos and the possibility of human rationality are co-ordinate.

We could not think at all if the world were not thinkable, if it had not intelligible structure, if it were not in some sense the embodiment of 'reason' or *logos*.

We can put it in two complementary ways. Since the cosmos is rational we can reason about it. Since human beings are rational animals, the world is a rational system, a 'realm' of reason and mind. Thinking is more than just we humans thinking. Thinking and knowing is the 'thought' in the world flowing into our thought The world reason or *nous* flows into our human knowing. To understand the world you have to understand *logos*, the instrument of exploration.[13]

---

13 Cf. J. H. Randall, *Aristotle*, pp. 102-4.

Logos is the instrument for the expression of knowledge. Aristotle's 'actual intellect' is actually *logos*. His 'actual intellect' is impersonal. It is immortal and eternal but has no memory. This was an early Platonic view. There are no personal undertones to the conception of *logos*.

Aristotle used the term 'beginning' for the first principles of the process of reasoning. He bequeathed to the world an elaborate system of knowledge. He proposed that to construct a system of thought you must have rational and unquestioned first principles. The Greek word for 'first principle' is *arche*, the plural *archai*. The first principles of a process of reasoning, the *archai*, are 'seen', intuited. You grasp them before you can start reasoning. Upon these *archai* you then can begin to build your system of thought, and come to an understanding of the world, of everything. This word *arche* is used in the preface to the gospel of *John*.

The Greek could understand well what *John* had written The *logos* (word) is the *arche* (first principle). It is the beginning of the existence of the world, of the existence of everything. That *John* quite explicitly states: 'without *logos* nothing was made that was made'. Moreover you only understand by means of *logos*, word, in this case, in the new Christian context, by means of the *logos* made flesh, Jesus Christ.

> 'To connect Jesus with this [Platonic] philosophical material at all is to make Jesus not just Saviour or Messiah in Jewish terms but to give him cosmic significance in Hellenic terms. Clearly John 1:1-18 intends to elevate Jesus into a cosmic role by relating him to the creation story of *Genesis* 1. It is by him and with him that the world was formed.'[14]

The Word 'dabar' in the Hebrew vocabulary

The Hebrews had their own special understanding of 'word.' For them word was spoken utterance. They knew that often when

---

14 Diogenes Allen, *Philosophy for Understanding Theology,* p. 73.

a word (= also a series of words and sentences) was spoken, the speaker intended it to have influence and waited to observe that influence. When he uttered the word he had an expectation of its result in influencing the hearer. The word once spoken could not be recalled and its effect could not be halted. It was a power in the real world. It was not just a series of ephemeral sounds.

The Hebrews were not speculative and philosophical as were the Greeks. Their outlook was practical and concrete. For the Hebrew the term 'word', *dabar,* denoted a living thing. It was much more dynamic and concrete than our Western term 'word.' As the speaker speaks his word, *dabar*, it becomes a living reality. It is an extension of the person who speaks, be he in ordinary life or be he prophet. Once the word is spoken, an action has been performed. To speak the word is to perform a deed. The human word, once spoken, goes out into the world and is productive and non-revocable. Isaac's blessing of Jacob once pronounced cannot be undone. Esau, whose right it was to receive that blessing, has lost it and must be given a different one.

> The living word comes to the prophets. It works. It is creative or destructive. God's word is an action. It produces an effect. He comes to his people with his word. He controls the word spoken and the effect it produces. When he comes to the prophets with his word, there is sometimes a vision. The vision passes, but the word pronounced remains. 'The decisive revelation is the word, not the vision. The word is creative. It is also sustaining.'[15]

It is also demanding. The hearer is called upon to make an appropriate response to the word he has heard. Israel is challenged to right action by the active delivering and hearing of the word.

For the devoted Jew the word was creative. He chanted: 'By the word of the LORD were the heavens made' (*Psalm.* 33:6). The

---

15 Th. C. Vriezen, *An Outline of Old Testament Theology,* p. 251. Cf. p. 239.

word was communicative. The great prophets had introduced their messages with the impressive claim, 'Thus saith the Lord'.

The Jew Philo of Alexandria (20 B.C.- 40 A.D.) brought together these key ideas of the Greeks and the Hebrews. Plato had spoken of the distinction between the ideal and the real. Philo knew this distinction and spoke of the world as the *logos* of God. He went a step further. 'He could identify the *logos* with the ideal man, first or primal man, God's image from whom all mortal men derive.' So, in drawing ideas from these two religious and philosophical cultures, *John* has provided himself with a means of effective communication with Jew and Greek, Christian and pagan, religious and profane alike.[16]

The logos as God's command

It is an error to claim that the *logos* is an idea in the mind of God, God's concept. Rather the *logos* is God's utterance not God's concept. It is not an inactive idea in the divine mind, placid and unaffected and unaffecting. To speak of it as concept recalls the Platonic version of 'creation' where the Idea, pre-existent and eternal is the subject. For Plato, the Idea is given form and change and cosmos result. The formula *creatio ab initio temporis* denies this Platonic notion of a pre-existent idea in the mind of God.

Rather for *John,* God knows himself in the *logos.* He knows himself in knowing the Son, and the ideas are then realised. For Plato, the creation is the decision that all or some of ideas in the mind of God shall be realised. Not for *John.* The Platonic concept can easily mislead us here. The act of creation is an act of communication, not an act enclosed in the deity. The Word of God is an utterance, an address. The address is a command. The *logos* is

---

16 Cf. John Marsh, *Saint John.* Harmondsworth: Pelican Books, 1971. pp. 100f.

God's command. 'God commands the world to be. This command is obeyed, and the act of obedience is the existence of the world.'[17]

Word as God's expression

God expresses himself and his expression is his 'Word.'
It is in encounter with the Word that creatures come to know God.
That knowledge is expressed in our limited human language.

It has by now become very clear that we encounter special difficulties when we try to speak of God. To confess him as 'Maker of heaven and earth' is a prime example. Here as elsewhere we are using personal terms of God. If we ask how we can say this and what it means to say this we immediately come to realise how difficult it is to speak in human terms about God, the only terms we have.

In the past God was often thought of as an object. He was conceived as one who could be approached and understood in terms derived from our experience of the world and made comprehensible by means of logical deduction and exposition, in short by thinking about him. In certain cases, it was believed, his existence could be demonstrated. So the conclusive arguments had to be produced.

But, though this has been the case, Christians came to understand that God is not an 'object'. Knowing this they manifest that knowledge by using personal terms of him. God is not an object within the cosmos. Therefore, if he is known at all, he will not be known as we know objects within our experience of the world. We come to our knowledge of such objects by observation, through sensation, by constructing arguments to conclusions. But God is transcendent and so those avenues are closed to limited human beings. So how is God to be known at all?

Should he become known, it will be because he performs acts whose description can be made in human language. He will be made known through the 'Word', but the grasping will be unique.

17 *Jenson, Systematic Theology.* Volume 2, pp. 6-7.

Here the important distinction is being made between the relation between expressing and knowing. God finds means of expression. The creature comes to read that expression and finds that it is the avenue to knowledge of God. That knowledge is then expressed in personal terms.

> Christians speak of God as Creator and Lord, 'who reveals and imparts his acts through the Word and who refers in the Word to his acts.

> ... one of the first things one learns on becoming a Christian is the distinction between the pictorial image and the divine reality to which the words and pictures point.[18]

It is because God has expressed himself and continues to express himself that God is known. A clear distinction is to be made between the divine reality, the form by which God is expressed, and the knowledge human beings acquire of him.

We speak of God in human language. The speaking is witness to the acts that God has performed and is performing. The language is of necessity drawn from our experience of the world as human subjects, and is therefore anthropomorphic language. Since we are is finite, we cannot transcend our finitude even in the use of the most abstruse and abstract language. God transcends the limitations of the world. We do not. So we do not come to the knowledge of God by employing the same means that are successful in knowing and understanding our world.

God is Creator. We are creatures. God in his freedom makes the approach to man and comes into the world, 'as the one who does not belong to the world.' In making this approach, the Creator also makes it possible for man to know him as he comes into the conditioned human and natural world in which we use human language. It is the coming to us in this way that makes words possible for us to express his coming. Without the prior act of God in such

---

18 Helmut Gollwitzer, *The Existence of God as Confessed by Faith*, pp. 147, 251

revealing activity there could be no authentic way of expressing the knowledge in our own human language, even if that should prove to be inadequate.

So we, the human creatures, cannot by observation, sensation and deduction, arrive at a knowledge of God. We use such methods in our successful search for knowledge within the cosmos, but they are not the ways that we can come to a knowledge of God. But as God reveals himself and the Word is grasped, the human can understand the expression by which the revelation is made possible and expressed. We never transcend the limitations of our language, even in speaking of the revealing act of God. We are creatures and our language is anthropomorphic. But that does not mean that there are not poorer and better ways of using our language! The very use of language should remind us that God is transcendent. He is Creator. We are creatures. Without the Word, we would know nothing of the transcendent God.

The term 'Word' thus has an important theological use, and the overtones of the biblical understanding of the gospel of *John* are ever present as it is employed theologically: 'the word was made flesh'.

5

CREATION AND PROVIDENCE

The term 'classical theism' refers to the content of a series of statements and treatments made by various representatives of the Christian church over the centuries. It suggests a broad agreement about what the belief in creation has meant to the Christian believer.

To define creation, according to classical theism, we include the continuing reality of what was brought into being 'in the beginning.' The terms 'Creator', 'creation' do not refer exclusively to the bringing into being of a world. The 'making' of all that is is not completed in the initial act. For the world once in being is a history. It moves through time to its completion in the eschaton. Meanwhile the events of our human history unfold century after century. The Christian church has recognised that God continues to maintain the world of his creation. The doctrine of creation includes the sustaining of that created world. Creation is not complete at the moment of its beginning. It reaches from the beginning to the consummation, the 'end', the *telos*. Creation awaits its fulfilment. The purpose of the Creator is yet to be realised. The whole course of history is yet incomplete. Within that history God's providence is an aspect of his creative activity. So we speak of this as 'continuous creation' *creatio continua.*

Representative statements about providence

That this has become part of the Christian understanding of
creation is clear from many expressions of Christian belief. We take
representative statements to illustrate. The Thirty-nine Articles and
the Westminster Confession are sample statements which make
clear that to confess that God is Creator includes the belief that he
sustains the creation by his providence. Creation has to do with the
preservation, sustaining, and direction of the world of the Creator.

The first of the **Thirty-Nine articles (1563)** states:

> There is but one living and true God, everlasting,
> without body, parts or passions; of infinite power,
> wisdom and goodness; the Maker, and Preserver of
> all things both visible and invisible.

The Westminster Confession (1646) The fourth and fifth
chapter states:

> IV. It pleased God the Father, Son, and Holy
> Ghost, for the manifestation of the glory of His eternal
> power, wisdom, and goodness, in the beginning, to
> create, or make of nothing, the world, and all things
> therein whether visible or invisible, in the space of six
> days; and all very good.

> V I. God the great Creator of all things does
> uphold, direct, dispose, and govern all creatures,
> actions, and things, from the greatest even to the least,
> by His most wise and holy providence, according to His
> infallible foreknowledge, and the free and immutable
> counsel of His own will, to the praise of the glory of
> His wisdom, power, justice, goodness, and mercy.

> V II. Although, in relation to the foreknowledge
> and decree of God, the first Cause, all things come

to pass immutably, and infallibly; yet, by the same providence, He orders them to fall out, according to the nature of second causes, either necessarily, freely, or contingently.

Calvin (1509-1564) had said:

'God is rightly acknowledged as the Creator of heaven and earth only while their perpetual preservation is ascribed to Him'.[19]

We put **contemporary statements** alongside:

'The world is no less dependent on God's creating word in any moment of its existence than it was at the beginning.'[20]

'The concept of God's continuing creation of the world in each succeeding moment of its passage is the ground for the further doctrine of God's providential rule over each aspect of creation in each moment of its duration.'[21]

Creation is not just the bringing into being of a cosmos. That 'bringing into being' is the expression of purpose in making human life possible. That purpose is yet to be fulfilled. To say that God creates the cosmos needs to be clarified by saying that the cosmos is a history, not simply a harmonious concatenation of material objects. God created possibility and that possibility is human history. God creates man and in so doing the openness that will mean choice and so the creation of history, something ongoing and yet to be fulfilled. Within that history there comes through God's revelation the understanding that history is purposive, that there is meaning, a *telos*, to that history. From within that history there is revealed the direction of that purpose and the means to its fulfilment and

19   *Commentary* on *Genesis* 2:2
20   Robert W. Jenson, *Systematic Theology, Volume 2.* p. 9.
21   Langdon Gilkey, *op. cit.*, p. 95.

consummation, in the person of Jesus Christ. Thus the doctrine of creation looks forwards to that completion.

So creation must encompass the whole of history and not talk only of the beginning. It must be forward looking, not with its attention exclusively to the past 'moment' of the emergence of the cosmos. It is thus through and through eschatological. Creation is not complete until the completion of history. That is yet to come. The completion will be God's work.

The corollaries to the teaching that God is independent is that his creatures are dependent, contingent beings and that the cosmos within which the creatures move and have their being is also likewise dependent. Human dependence means human frailty. Were not God to sustain that frail being, it would no longer exist. God's creation continues in the world. so the world does not revert to non-being.

So arises the paradox of God's immanence, i.e. his active presence within the creation. The paradox results when we attempt to coordinate the claim that God is transcendent, other, but not 'wholly other' than his creatures, with the claim that he is immanent, actively present within the creation. God is both transcendent, active beyond history, and immanent, active within history. How shall we coordinate these two apparently paradoxical claims?

God is not 'other' in the sense that there is no question of his relation to his creature. He is not 'wholly other'. Were he *wholly* other than his creatures there could be no talk of relating to them. This would be a kind of absolute deism qualified at one point, the point of the beginning of the cosmos, God having no further relation to the world of his creation except at the initial stage of bringing it into being. But it is not necessary to maintain such an extreme deistic position on the transcendence of God.

God in his freedom created human beings dependent, but free. As creator he is both different from us and involved with us. The Christian makes his central assertion in identifying the coming of Jesus Christ as the activity of the Creator God, 'above' the world and yet active within the world. Only a transcendent God could 'redeem' his 'fallen' creatures. The Redeemer is the Creator. This is the basis for the Christian teaching of providence.

So there is significance in the paradoxical statement that God created the world in order to redeem it. The revelation of God's love in the 'sending' of the Son is the central act of God's creative activity. Here we reach the heart of the doctrine of creation.

Any Christian talk about creation must begin with Jesus Christ and that means that it takes place within the context of faith. Such talk concerns the whole of history as 'world'. Such talk will be about God. Creation is about God. We talk about God not in the abstract way of natural theology (so-called), but in relation to the God revealed in Jesus Christ, the *Logos*, the Word. Such talk of God as the 'Maker of Heaven and Earth,' and 'the Father of Jesus Christ' comprehends the whole of human history and the end to which it, as God's creation is leading, as the unique subject-matter. We are not confined to talking about six days but to the whole of reality, time, history, even eternity!

> 'It has always been of decisive importance for Christianity that the God who liberates and redeems through Jesus Christ is none other than the creator of the world . . . . If the Christian God cannot be understood as the creator of the world, my personal experience of being indebted to him for everything can well be pious self-deception.'[22]

The Question: How?

What are we asking for when we ask the question 'How?' Just what are we asking when we ask, How does Mrs. Jones make a cake? How does the upholsterer make an easy chair? How does the scientist make an electronic telescope? How does the seed become a plant?

The answer anyone will give is that you bring together certain elements in a way that can in principle be described, if not ob-

22   Wolfhart Pannenberg, *The Apostles Creed*. London; S. C. M. Press Ltd., 1972. p. 36

served. You put component ingredients in order in a certain way. It may be very simple to do, but very hard to learn. A child finds it takes effort to make a box and later a machine. A scientist works for years to isolate a certain vaccine.

We shall often put the question in another way. Observing an event or an object we may well ask, 'What has caused that?' For we believe that nothing happens without a cause. So the 'How' question is often satisfactorily answered by detailing preceding events and singling out one or more as the necessary conditions for what has taken place or what has been produced.

We often witness something being produced. So we conclude that there must always be an answer to the question 'How?', even if it is inaccessible to the observer, or even if the explanation as to the procedure is quite beyond our understanding. Even if we can't observe the process, or even understand it, we are certain that there is an answer to the question, 'How?' and that it will consist in putting necessary elements and events together in a certain way. Both the detective and the scientist know that that is often a complicated procedure.

So when we speak of creation as originating and sustaining the universe, we may find it an insuperable puzzle, an unanswerable question as to *how* God has done it and is doing it. We cannot observe the processes involved in the action of God. We have no access to a preceding transcendent set of necessary and sufficient conditions. So we cannot describe them. How then can we give some content to the statement that God acts to sustain and provide for his creation and creatures? The 'how', it would seem, is quite beyond us.

Intermediaries

We may say, as did John Milton, in his short poem, *On his Blindness*, that God has intermediaries that he is constantly despatching to do his will in the cosmos, as well as myriads standing by in reserve for such service.

'his State
Is Kingly. Thousands at his bidding speed
And post o're Land and Ocean without rest:
They also serve who only stand and waite.'

Or, to put it in the language the simple believer sometimes uses: God sends an angel to answer my prayer for protection, for healing, for sustenance whether I pray for myself or for others.

But that does not relieve us, now that we have begun to inquire whether there is any point in asking the question, 'How?' For since God is working through an intermediary we then have to inquire also about the go-between and ask how that intermediary does it. But asking 'How?' was our original problem. The simple believer will just say, 'I do not know how!' and go on with his sincere affirmation of divine intervention. We may share his attitude by responding: 'Are we not trying to talk about something we know nothing about?'

But there is more. The biblical account speaks of God as punishing and rewarding. The Israelites will be punished if they are disobedient, sinful, and recalcitrant. The righteous will be rewarded if they obey. The great empires of the ancient world were the instruments on that retribution.

In contrast to this the psalmist happily declared, 'I have been young, and now am old; yet have I not seen the righteous forsaken, nor his seed begging bread.' *Psalm* 37: 25.

We can only conclude that his experience must have been extremely limited or that his feeling of security must have made him blind to what was taking place. None of us would be able to make such a confession, given our ordinary experience of life and of the extraordinary outrages of our centuries.

Intervention

Intervention means the introduction of a new factor into an already existing system so that what results would otherwise not in fact have come about. We usually employ the term for special kinds of situation. Mother intervenes to end the children's quarrel. The police intervene to quell a riot. We sometimes hear, 'If someone doesn't do something, nothing will change.' But someone does something and things do change. Intervening makes a difference.

When we apply the term to natural events, we mean usually that an original or intermediary initiates an action by modifying the situation. This modification, addition or subtraction, makes a difference to what would otherwise have been a predictable outcome, given the original situation. We then change the prediction. Many would have died of malaria had not the authorities put appropriate materials into the mosquitoes' breeding grounds environment. They did. So that was the cause of the beneficial outcome.

Many Christians, like John Milton, readily understand the despatch of intermediaries to carry out the divine will in the world. They believed that without such intervention a quite different course of events, or in the particular case, a quite different state of affairs would have obtained. They teach their children about their guardian angel who will protect them from harm. They learn how an angel delivered Peter from prison. They may also believe that an angel has saved their loved one from harm.

Some events, for example a sudden improvement in a seriously ill patient's condition, seem inexplicable in terms of the normal course of natural events. When this happens the reaction is one of great relief mingled with puzzlement. But for the believer there is something else. The happy family give thanks to God for the recovery for it was a beneficial one for them. They often will say, 'If God had not intervened, we should have lost our loved one.'

So let us consider this belief, 'If God had not intervened . . . .' The problem is that there is no identification mark of God's intervening, as there would always be in the human case — say when the doctor had intervened as he experimented with a new drug. She would be able to give an exact account of what she had done, answering the question, 'What did you do to produce this welcome but unexpected result?' If God intervened the only trace would be an unusual and unexpected concatenation of events and of objects. In the case of divine providence the course of nature proceeds as usual. Everything appears as normal, and there is no accounting apart from the ordinary empirical one, in this case a medical one. We are well able, in principle, to identify a human intervention. But we cannot identify a divine one. We cannot indicate the initiating event that was the cause of the unexpected result. We are simply left to say that the result was unexpected. So we say 'It was a miracle', by that meaning that we cannot explain it. It was divine intervention, but we cannot say how. Intervention by a divine agent cannot be identified by ordinary empirical means. It remains a confession of faith.

In the normal course of explaining an out of the ordinary event we can isolate the intervening events and explain their presence as the cause of the result we witnessed. The believer cannot do this for the divine. He can only account for the event in normal cause-effect terms. He cannot go beyond the empirical to some transcendent cause and say, We have isolated it, as in the case of the doctor's activity and materials. When the angel intervening does not leave a trace. We may track the human agent and the means that agent introduced. We cannot track the divine agent and the means employed. If God intervened, the only observables would be a concatenation of events reacting normally in a predicable way, but producing an unexpected result. That God had set them in motion would not be discoverable.

So suddenly the wind stops and the crew of the ship were saved from disaster. That was a unique event. If the natural event was unusual, one can point to its uniqueness, even sometimes calling that natural event or coincidence of events a miracle and then saying, 'God's hand was in this.' Surprise at the unexpected outcome leads to joy, and joy seems to demand gratitude, so the believer is grateful to God. Thus it seems obvious that one should speak of God intervening.

We are happy when what seems like extraordinary events produce an outcome that is productive of human well-being. We would hardly do so if the result were otherwise, as in the case of my unfortunate student killed while logging. We would then say that it was sheer unfortunate coincidence, with emphasis on the assessment as 'unfortunate.' That is because it did not produce human well-being. Otherwise one might hear it said that it was the will of God which we must bear bravely and in faith. But that then seems to assume that the damaging events were in some sense God's responsibility. Speaking of the will of God 'allowing' does not mean the same for the believer as saying that God initiated the event. So arises the distinction between initiating and permitting. That is a problem we shall not discuss further.

The counter instance

Take the case of an unexpected event, a 'non repeatable counter instance' to what we anticipated. The religiously inclined may call it a 'miracle'. But 'miraculous' may simply mean 'astonishing', not that every counter instance will be something that produces wonder. Such instances take place in different contexts for ordinary mortals in their normal living of day to day life, as well as for scientists experiencing and investigating phenomena in many and varied contexts. Scientists meet with these counter instances that resist their understanding and know how to deal with them constructively. They believe that while they may not be able to give an explanation now, they may be able to do so in the future. The counter instance is not in principle inexplicable. We go on living, working, waiting, asking questions, and investigating. Some day we may find an explanation. We have evidence that something is resistant to our understanding which we are at present unable to explain. We serve the cause of rationality by waiting.

Interruption, Interference

Whatever providence means, whatever intervention means cannot mean interruption. There is no gate crashing into nature. There is no suspension of the laws of nature, no annihilation of the continuing reality of its order. Just think what that would mean. The interference *per impossibile* with nature would mean suspension of the order of nature. That would mean its destruction. There can be such modifying of the laws of nature when the raging of the ocean overwhelms the boat, no holding in abeyance of the natural order when the striking of an iceberg is about to destroy the boat and the human beings in it, no modifying the operation of poison when someone swallows it, no disturbing the revolution of the earth to make the sun appear to stand still (*pace* Joshua), no neutralising the effect of gravity when someone you love has jumped out of the sixth story window. Such suspension of natural order would mean chaos. It would involve the annihilation of all system and rationality.

Sustaining

We shall now examine further the idea of 'sustaining', the term used in the creed. From your experience and mine we know that to sustain something means continually to be in active touch or to maintain an influence with what we are sustaining. If I am to sustain the life of my children, grow some crops in my garden, or simply to sustain my good health, I must be continuously initiating whatever is appropriate. I must provide for continuous assistance.

To produce a new result or even to maintain the status quo requires that I do something, that I keep setting something up, that I produce or maintain a cause or set of causes to achieve the effect I desire. I initiate one event or series of events so I can produce another. I make one event or series of events to coincide with another. In this sense everything is co-incidence. But, of course, not every event that precedes or coincides with another is the cause of that other event. The coordination might be quite accidental. People knock off work when the whistle blows at five o'clock. But the one is not the cause of the other. For this A to be the cause of that B, this A must be in necessary not accidental connection with that B. The connection between the events must be a necessary one for us to say that A, the one event, is the cause or one of the causes of the B, the other.

We can express this by saying: 'If A had not happened B would not have happened. Such a principle is called a counterfactual. We can apply it quite simply. If mum had not taken the medicine, she would not have got better. We may then probe a little, by detailing how the doctor prescribed, what the medicine was, and its physical effect. That will satisfy us, even if we do not get around to talking about mum's having to be persuaded to take the stuff. If the deceased had not drunk the coffee, he would still be alive. If I had stayed at home, I would not have got knocked down. If my student had not gone logging, he would not have been killed. If he had stayed put when he heard the shout of 'Timber!' he would have survived. But by pointing out one counterfactual or by focussing only on one event we may not have found the cause. For every event is the result of many causes, not all of them contemporary, some even beyond the range of our possible investigation. It is a complicated business sometimes to discover which is the real cause, the crucial state of affairs, or event. In fact many events come together, one of which we usually single out as *the cause*. And we can go behind the impersonal events to the initiation of those events by the human will to produce them. Of course poison in a drink will cause death. But that is not all that is to be said. A villain causes the death by initially willing to provide the means to cause it.

It is very difficult to find out and describe what we might call the one and essential, basic, cause. Shall we say it is personal, the murderer's decision or physical, the cyanide? Of course it is both. We can readily discover and explain on the physical level and not even begin to track down or even understand the other personal (shall we call it the 'higher') level of cause. Knowing all the physical facts possible may not enable us to know the human cause. In addition to impersonal events in the cosmos, we have to reckon with the human will, personal planning, and the carrying out of human resolve. We are sometimes successful in accomplishing this. But it sometimes proves elusive. We are aware of the physical causes. Often that is all, the best that we can do.

What is the relevance of this for our discussion of providence?

Apply this to the idea of God's causing, i.e. initiating and sustaining, events within the cosmos. We are well able to note how it comes about that tsunamis cause death and destruction. We know quite well the physical details of how mum's taking the medicine resulted in her becoming fit. But the more remote cause is frequently hidden from us. In the human case we may be able to uncover it. Did she decide to take it, or not? Was it put in her food by someone concerned and sympathetic, but unbeknown to her? Here we can talk about sympathy, decision, intention, motivation, and activity.

How can we connect a transcendent God to a particular series of co-incidental physical events within the cosmos? For examples, take Mum's recovery thought of as an answer to prayer, and take Dad's avoidance of an automobile accident he believes was the result of angelic intervention. It is no wonder that God is well spoken of as the 'hidden' God. It is faith that interprets the event as miraculous or as providential.

In one sense everything is 'coincidence'. For everything is the result of things coming together. The word is usually used of unusual and inexplicable or unexplained events. Every event is an effect and has an effect. We know and always work on the principle that in every case, every effect requires a cause. Our understanding of how things happen in the world consists in finding the appropriate event, or series of events as their cause. We explain what causes what when we select and deliberately bring this and that together, in a quite specific way. To explain the detail of the bringing together by analysing the concept of causation, we must leave to the philosopher to elucidate.

So we return to our quest, to throw light if possible on the claim that God maintains and directs events within the world. This is a problem because the Christian theist claims that God is supreme, that he transcends the world. How then can he be somewhat immanent within it? Deism places God above and beyond the world both spatially, temporarily, and logically. But the Christian theist rejects that absolute independence.

Independence

The theist confesses God's independence of the world in the initial act of creating it and then goes on to speak of his acting within the world. Nevertheless the theist wishes to preserve the independence of the world from the Creator and Sustainer. That enables him to recognise that events in the world have their own independence. God is not the initiator of everything that happens in the cosmos. The claim sounds paradoxical.

The paradox can be stated bluntly:

God is provident within the cosmos.

God is independent of the cosmos.

Immanence is somehow to be combined with transcendence. If you emphasise the independence of the cosmos, the transcendence will be reduced to a 'tinge' that seems to need further explanation rather than providing elucidation. But if no elucidation is forth-coming, we might simply be told, 'It is a mystery! After all we are dealing with matters which take us to the very edge and perhaps beyond the scope of our knowledge.' At this point we may become agnostic.

The paradox must be maintained to preserve the belief that God acts within the world, hears and answers prayer. An alternative is simply to say that the world is quite independent of God, that it runs according to a rational order, a *logos*, and that no interven-tion is either needed or possible. No such confession of continual sustaining, involving intervention, is needed or is even possible. If the believer wishes to speak of providence and miracle, he is inter-preting events in the world in a religious way, a way demanded by his religious experience.

But there is a problem in saying the cosmos is independent. For that term demands a relationship. Independent of what? Well! Independent of God of course! To speak of the need for a 'tinge of deism' seems to suggest that the theist wants it both ways. He wants to say more than that God initiated the cosmos and then left it to itself and less than that he intervenes or might intervene within it to produce appropriate effects. Certainly he does not entertain the idea of the total self-sufficiency of the world, however difficult it is to understand the theistic point of view.

At any rate the theist is not called upon to do the impossible, to explain the 'how' of providence as continuous sustaining any more than called upon to explain the 'how' of the initial creation. He may simply assert that the world of second causes is the world of God's creation. Theology must allow the scientist, in fact leave it to the scientist, to explain and explore 'second causes'. The second part of this book examines this problem in terms of the role of the scientist and that of the theologian. It examines clear statements of representative leading theologians.

The doctrine of creation affirms Jesus Christ as the expression of God, and this enables us to see the cosmos as God's world because of the revelation in Jesus Christ. Man's place in all of this is to treat the world as creation and to take a part in caring for the cosmos. This is certainly provided for in the *Genesis* text where 'man', i.e. the human creature ('Adam' = man) = the human creature), is given the task of tending to the earth and producing fruit from it.

6

CREATION AND EVIL

Evil exists. It is a reality in the cosmos, the ordered world. Evil is present and persisting in the world of human experience It is a disturbance and so needs explaining. Dualism was an early and persistent attempt to provide an explanation. The god of light and the god of darkness are in ceaseless conflict. So evil results and continues as in the Persian religion Ormuzd and Ahriman are in perpetual battle. Here evil and good are the two ultimate principles made concrete as deities. The basic principle of dualism is that evil co-exists in opposition with good within the cosmos.

Theism holds that the Creator is good and that creation is the product of his goodwill. The Christian recognises the ubiquitous presence of evil in the world, but speaks of its ultimate destruction and offers immediate salvation. But an acceptable rational explanation has still to be given. For the Christian God, conceived on the analogy with finite persons, has concern and care for creatures who feel the presence of evil within and without.

Evil is no illusion. Evil is real. So its presence poses a serious problem when it is held that the world is, at least potentially, a good world, that it is God's world. The Christian theist believes that 'this is my father's world', that the creatures are good and that the purpose for the creation is good. So the presence of evil is a particular problem because of the claim that God cares for the creature, not only in the sense that all will be well in the future, but that all is well in the here and now of our often painful existence. Cf. *Romans* 8:22, 28.

The sources of evil are twofold. Each of these pose a problem for the Christian theist.

(1) the human creatures misuse their freedom and evil results and proliferates.

Since human beings sometimes employ their freedom to produce constructive results, would it not have been possible for them to have been created so that they would always employ that freedom in a positive way? Or, if that were not possible, is this the best possible world that God could have created? Why could not the Creator have given his creatures such freedom that they would always employ that freedom well, for the good?

For the theist, to say that God created *ex nihilo* means that God is responsible for everything that exists. It is then a matter of distinguishing the different meanings of 'responsibility'. Is it a solution to say that God created human beings as agents, secondary agents within the creation, and must take responsibility for that. If it is their exercise of freedom that causes the evil, God is not *directly* responsible for that.

(2) Natural causes produce both physical and mental pain.

We find that some natural events promote human well-being, and are constantly looking for the co-ordination of events, objects, and phenomena that will do so. We are also well aware of other phenomena that threaten or destroy that well-being. We are constantly looking for ways of counteracting and destroying such causes. But there would be no ordered system or ordered life at all if predictable results did not occur from the existence of natural order. But those results are not always hospitable to human values. Given certain conditions, droughts are inevitable. Given other conditions, bountiful harvests can be expected. One is antithetic to human well-being. The other is productive of it. There could be neither without the ordered system. Intervention within the system would totally disrupt its order and so make human life impossible. We must all die. We may enjoy a multitude of life's pleasures and satisfactions. Our death is to be anticipated as a result of the participation we experience within the system. That participation brings us both grief and joy. We may regret the one and rejoice on account of the other. We hope we may learn to live constructively with both, and we strive constantly to so.

It is difficult, indeed impossible, for us to conceive how it would have been possible for a world to exist in which nature always served the interests of the human and so always promoted human well-being. We might think we can imagine such a world. But we cannot conceive it.

We must simply confront it. There are then two levels that engage us as we confront the evil. We have to face the pains, the 'slings and arrows of outrageous fortune' of our lives. We must come to terms with it in our experience: disease, disaster, and finally death. We also think about it and ask questions about its existence. It is on the one hand an existential problem, personal and communal. It is on the other a philosophical one. We think about it and attempt to understand and explain it.

For the monist evil is an illusion. We escape evil by becoming united with the One. It is because of our ignorance that we speak of evil. It is because we are not aware of our identity with the whole. So in our ignorance we talk about evil. Human existence being limited and finite is itself evil. But there is a remedy. If we start off with that conviction the problem seems to disappear. But its apparent disappearance does not mean that the problem has been solved. The logic may seem satisfactory, but the evil has still to be endured. A satisfactory explanation must deal with evil on both the levels existential as well as philosophical.

For the dualist, evil has its source in matter.

For the naturalist evil is due to the blind working of natural forces beyond human control. So we must resign ourselves to the inevitable. In different senses evil is a permanent feature of finite existence as we know and experience it.

For the Christian theist a personal God cares for his creation in the here and now. God has communicated to us by coming into the world and, in the person of Jesus, sharing in our suffering and taking death upon himself. The Christian answer to the problem of evil lies here, and in the confession of resurrection. It constitutes a response to the problem of evil. But it is not an 'explanation'. For to explain evil would be to excuse it.

The transcendent God and secondary Agents

The concept of God the Creator is of a non-material, self existent, transcendent being. To 'create' means to 'bring about existence'. To say, 'God created the world 'means God, *alone*, brought about the existence of all things apart from himself. The claim that God is the Creator of the 'world,' the 'universe,' is that God created everything other than himself. After the creation God is not alone. There are 'secondary agents'. In their turn the system that God created and the beings within it produce effects. The craftsman produces the building. The scientist produces the antibiotic. The dictator initiates the massacre. The sun makes the flowers to grow. Volcanoes produce destruction and suffering. The world changes as these and myriad other processes take place.

The created order has an independence from the Creator. The created beings have a freedom and the created system has an order. This is the product of the creator's intention. God brings it about that agents other than he can bring about events he does not directly initiate, within a system of nature that is regular and predictable. He intended and brought that system into being.

So 'God created' has been given two interpretations. Here a choice has to be made. Is God's action necessary for things to continue in existence, once created, or does the initial emergence of the system of things carry within itself the dynamic for its own continuance? Does God continue his creative activity within the system he created? If so, does that mean that whatever happens within the creation is an example of the immediate activity of the Creator? Two alternatives present themselves.

(1) God initiated and sustains all that exists. He causes the sun to shine when it does shine and the planets to move with regularity. He produces the chemical and biological reactions that take place in their uncounted trillions every second. An omnipresent spirit

is the creator of all things which exist and come to exist within the cosmos What takes place in the world has its causes in the direct, continuing creative activity of the Creator. This came to be known as *direct providence* in Christian doctrine and *occasionalism* in philosophy.

(2) God brought about an initial state through his basic 'act', in which events within the system cause other events. That God created a system, a universe, means he initiated the operation of natural laws. The whole is dependent on the creator for its initial existence. Thereafter events within the system are self-sustaining. Nature with its 'natural laws' exists as the product of creation. So there is independence from God.

One of the basic problems for the Christian theist is to conceive what it means to say God acts. Christians must respond to the question of God's relation to the creation, to the questions: Does the claim 'God created' mean that he keeps the universe in being, that if he did not sustain it continuously it would cease to exist? Does he sustain it at every moment of its existence? Must we, taking one step further, hold that in some way God is present in the decisions of the rational creatures and their consequences? Is the idea of God sustaining creation continuously the belief that the individual's acts, causes and effects within the system are also God's direct acts? What does the distinction between direct and indirect acts of God mean?

Or must we conceive God's action in some other way, as indirect, mediated? Or alternatively, shall we simply assert it and then be silent even thinking that there might be a very different notion and operation of cause and effect here, not knowable to us? Christians are interested not only or even exclusively in beginnings, but also in the end time, the eschaton. The fulfilment of creation and the understanding of the complex history within the creation will be revealed at the end. Meanwhile God is directing events according to his will. Some Christian communities place great emphasis on the fulfilment of prophecy, thus specifying the particular manner in which God is operating in the affairs of man and will continue to operate until the creation of the 'new earth.'

The belief that God has control over the events of human history entails that he directs the events of human history as his providence indicates best. We might focus on predictions about the end-time in particular. God will destroy when he wills. God will create a new heaven and a new earth when he wills. He acts in the affairs of men to bring the world to its final consummation. He will, therefore, cease to maintain the present order in its being when he deems it appropriate and will bring about a new order, a 'new heavens and a new earth'.

Assumptions about the fulfilment of prophecy demand that this be so. It is logically forbidden to deny that God is 'behind' events in that universe within which human agents exercise and effect their wills. Not only is God constantly initiating events in that universe, He also provides clues by means of his prophets, to those who can understand them, how the course of history will turn out. To deny that God is 'behind' it all would, for many Christians, seem logically forbidden. But *how* we may conceive the uninterrupted direction at every moment by an omnipresent deity within the overall sustenance of the universe remains problematic. How can we provide a reasonable account of the sustenance, even predestination, of human wills and actions? For within this creation, human agents exercise and effect their wills so that their effects are not the direct result of God's agency.

Second Causes

The Westminster Confession (1646) speaks of 'second causes'. Much was happening in the seventeenth century in science and philosophy. A new age had dawned with the scientific revolution and the church was taking some notes. It was the century in which Isaac Newton (1642-1727) produced his great mathematical and physical system. René Descartes (1596-1650) defended a mechanical understanding of the universe and John Locke (1632-1704) had developed an empirical philosophy deeply indebted to the advances in scientific understanding.

While earlier church statements had clearly announced that God was the Sustainer of the universe, its proponents knew nothing of the scientific advances later to come, and so simply did not have the sophisticated concept of 'second causes' that was later developed. Since they knew nothing of them, they did not have to explain providence in relation to second causes. They could not have known about them. Once the concept emerged, along with a quite revolutionary idea of the unity and rationality of world, explicated in mathematical terms, and once it had given rise to intense exploration and speculation, new challenges rose for the believers to explain their belief. We must now do that in the light both of the new knowledge of the universe and in the light of discussions about causality that emerged as philosophers thought about the scientific method that had produced the new knowledge.

It is to be noted that in the Westminster Confession 'Preserver' and 'Maker' are set together as complementary subjects. God's agency as 'Preserver' is an aspect of his agency as 'Creator'. In making the confession of providence the framers acknowledged the newly understood order of nature. That is the point of the reference to 'second causes'.

We are now in a very different cultural context from that of the Middle Ages, when Thomas Aquinas (A. D. 1225-1274) spoke of God as 'First Cause' as the conclusion of an argument from Effect to Cause. The ground of this was the notion that every event within the cosmos requires a cause. That was the premise of the argument. He argued from the idea of cause within the cosmos to a First Cause. He proposed that this was a necessary logical step from the idea of cause within the cosmos. Having done this, and in doing so his 'First Cause' still remaining within the cosmos, he drew a further conclusion. His great leap was then to identify the 'First Cause', in the conclusion he drew from his argument, with the God of the Christian tradition. Having deduced that the 'first cause' was required to ground the system of causes in the cosmos,

he then in conclusion identified that 'first cause' with God, the
God of Christian tradition, the God who transcended the natural
system. That concluded the argument.

But what emerged as the conclusion of the argument was the
'philosopher's god'. Aquinas' First Cause' is an entity within the
system of causes, but not transcendent to it. By pointing out that
the god which is a 'first cause' is not 'the God of Abraham, Isaac,
and Jacob but 'the god of the philosopher', was the way Pascal
(1623-1662) dismissed the argument as failing to provide a proof
of the God of religious faith.

So the term 'second cause' needs some explanation. It refers
to what occurs in the order of nature where relations between phenomena and events are connected in terms of causes and effects. For
example, we explain growth of plants and of animals by speaking
of nutrition and trace growth in particular cases by indicating what
hinders and encourages it. We do so by making reference to quite
specific physical elements and conditions.

The enterprise of science as the organised examination of complex relations in the orderly world takes success for granted, success
in tracing and explaining cause-effect relations. It even welcomes
failure by acknowledging the importance of falsification in its quest.
It proceeds independently of any religious interest or beliefs. The
system of causes and effects with which science deals is autono-
mous. It is of this system we speak now when we talk of 'second
causes'.

The confession states the belief that while nature is an independent realm of such 'second causes', the whole 'falls out' according
to the divine will. That means that whatever happens within the
system may be said to be the product of the will of God. The purpose of confessions is to express accepted beliefs and convictions
and thereby to define them as acceptable. The confession then
leaves whatever problems arise in thinking about these statements
to the theologian to consider and to explain. That problem is to
elucidate how we shall conceive the independence of nature in
relation to the sustaining providence of God. The problem then is

to elucidate, if possible, the relation between God's transcendence and immanence.

God's transcendence is needed to account for his being an object worthy of worship. God's immanence is needed to account for faith in his continuing activity within the world.

To say that God's creativity is responsible for everything that exists seems in some way to involve the Creator in the mesh of human causality. If that is so, there could be a direct analogy with human causality. We have no other model. To say that God is cause *within* the cosmos is to speak of something fundamentally different from finite causes *within* the cosmos. For God is transcendent. All causes we know anything at all about are derived from our observation and experience within the system. But God is 'above' the system. We are 'within' it. Between the 'above' and 'within' is an impassable gulf. Is it even illuminating to speak in such spatial terms alone?

God as Creator and Sustainer is confessed as pre-eminent causality. That distinguishes him from the world. If God were not such supreme causality he would be indistinguishable from the world. But if he is supreme causality then knowledge of his causation is beyond human investigation. The Christian may confess it but he cannot investigate it. He confesses it for the simple reason that he has experienced the presence of God within the world. He is left with his affirmation of the paradox of God's transcendence and immanence. We may explain the 'how' of finite causation. But we cannot explain the 'how' of divine causation.

Addendum: Some Terms

The problem is to understand the relation between the initial creative act of bringing the world into existence and the claim that God's creative act continues by his maintaining the world in being and by initiating events within it. How shall we understand the relation between the initial creative act of God which produced the cosmos and the ongoing events theists regard as God's continuing act of conservation?

We look now at some definitions and explanations we need to clarify any satisfactory answer we give to the question, How is God now related to the cosmos? How are we to account for events, objects, processes in the cosmos? We may now sum up very briefly in general terms. the answers that have been given.

Classical Theism. God created a structured universe and continues to sustain it in being. The question is, How shall we conceive this? How are the two activities to be conceived and related. Here are the alternatives.

Atheism. God is not needed to explain the cosmos, either its origin or its continuance. The cosmos has an independent structure and so we can account for everything by reference to that structure. The account will be naturalistic, not requiring reference to any thing outside the structure.

Deism. God created a structured universe that after the creative act is quite independent and operates of its own resources. Thus there is no room for conservation by the divine originator. God needs to do nothing more to conserve the universe in being.

Transitional conservation. A form of deism. God's conservations, so to speak, occur at a distance. What takes place in the cosmos is a product of God's original act of creation. An illustration of an at-a-distance influence or creation would be such as the following.

The first event causes a second event. The second event causes a third (and the process could continue almost indefinitely.) So logically the first event is the cause of the third. We can represent this in logical terms:

A causes B

B causes C

Therefore: A causes C.

Occasionalism. God causes to happen whatever happens within the universe. God is responsible both for the coming into being of every particular thing and for every feature of every particular thing. What this implies is that we exclude any attempt to explain by means of innate causes.

Two explanations of the existence of the world appear as extreme and unsatisfactory for the Christian theist.

Deism holds that God's action is confined to the initial creative act. When once he has brought the world into being it continues in virtue of its structure and so has no further need for divine activity to maintain it in being.

Occasionalism is directly opposed to such a position and holds that God is active in everything that takes place, bringing about whatever is and continues to be within the cosmos. Some versions of the doctrine of providence embraced such a view. 'God sees the little sparrow fall.' Other theists find difficulty with it and would think of providence as God's initiation of some events selected from the whole, thus maintaining the divine activity and the initiating freedom of the human and the structured system of nature. Some such events are called miracles.

Pantheism

God and cosmos are identical. Cosmos emanates from God. God is not transcendent. Emanation replaces creation.

Panentheism

The cosmos is contained within the being of God who is not external to nature. But he is not identical with the natural processes. The world is not the totality of God. So pantheism and deism are rejected. God is continuously at work creating through the processes of the natural order. Dualism is also rejected with the assertion that while God is infinitely more than the universe, he is constantly working within it. The new is constantly emerging. So God is not responsible for evil.[23]

---

23 For a detailed discussion of these topics cf. Jonathan Kranvig, 'Creation and Conservation'. *Stanford Encyclopaedia of Philosophy*. This article provides a suggestion while examining the alternatives but concludes that a solution is yet to be found to the problem.

BIBLIOGRAPHY FOR PART I

Allen. Diogenes, *Philosophy for Understanding Theology*. London: S.C.M. Press, 1985.

Aristotle, M*etaphysics*, 1072a 20, 26.

Farley. Edward, *The Transcendence of God*. London: Epworth Press, 1962.

Gilkey. Langdon, Ma*ker of Heaven and Earth*. New York: Doubleday and Company, 1959.

Gollwitzer. Helmut, *The Existence of God as Confessed by Faith*. Translated by James W. Leitch. Philadelphia: The Westminster Press, 1965.

Jenson. Robert W., *Systematic Theology. Volume 2, The Works of God*. Oxford: University Press, 1999.

Kranvig. Jonathan, 'Creation and Conservation'. *Stanford Encyclopaedia of Philosophy*.

Marsh. John, *Saint John*. Harmondsworth: Pelican Books, 1971.

Pannenberg. Wolfhart, *The Apostles Creed*. London: S.C.M. Press Ltd., 1972.

Randall. J. H., *Aristotle*, New York: Columbia University Press, 1960.

Schleiermacher. Friedrich, *The Christian Faith*. Edinburgh: T. & T.
    Clark, 1976.

Thomas Aquinas, *Summa Theologica*, Question 2 Article 3. *Q. 46
    Art.1, Reply objections 8, 10.*

Vriezen, Th.C. *An Outline of Old Testament Theology*,
    Massachusetts: Branford Company, 1960.

CREATION: DISCUSSION QUESTIONS

INTRODUCTION

1 What makes Christian statements about God unique?

2 What can the Christian say about God and creation that the Hebrew cannot?

3 When does talk about the origin of the universe have religious significance?

4 How can a claim about creation be at the same time a statement of Christian faith?

5 In what specific ways did the scriptural writers understand the universe differently from us? Why is the difference important?

6 Is the story of creation in *Genesis* a Christian story?

I

FAITH AND SCIENCE

1 Define 'creationism'.

2 Why is there such opposition to creationism?

3 Are scientific questions and answers different from religious, theological ones?

4 How do you know when the form of the writing is narrative, Scripture is making an historical claim and when it is not?

5 Is there one essential thing about the *Genesis* account of creation? If you think so what is it?

6 Theology (confession of faith in God) is not physics. Is this not obvious? Discuss.

II

TWO QUESTIONS

1   How and why does a physical account of the origin of the physical universe differ from a believer's understanding of creation?

2   Why did the writer in our text say that a literal account of the origin of the physical universe has no relevance to the believer's confession that God created?

3   Recount Plato's 'probable tale'. Do you find something positive in his attitude?

4   How can we give an account of the relation between time and eternity? Between dependent being and self-sustaining, transcendent being?

5   Since faith cannot disagree with science in the name of faith, but only in the name of science, then the disagreement is not theology. Discuss.

III

ANALOGY

1   Give a definition of anthropomorphism, analogy.

2   Think of several different kinds of example where human features are applied to non-human things.

3   Distinguish personal ideas of God from impersonal ones. Find and explain specific examples.

4   Since God transcends the universe how does language about the universe apply to him? Consider the analogy of the watch maker.

5   Why are we unable to prove the existence of God?

6   How do stories function if they do not always have a literal reference?

7   How is a religious believer interested in literal physical descriptions of the solar system and of the universe beyond it?

8   What does the idea of 'Creator', 'Maker' suggest? Is it presumptuous to speak of God by using such an idea, or is it simply meaningless.

9   What is the intention of the phrase 'creation out of nothing'?

10 Why was, and is, the idea of the eternal cycle of time attractive?

11 What does it mean to say that the beginning is linked to the end ?

IV

WORD

1   The word is God's command. The word is God's expression. So are related to creation. Explain.

2   'The word became flesh'. What does this say about creation?

3   'The Word was in the beginning' How does the Greek understanding of beginning, *arche,* illuminate this?

V

PROVIDENCE

1 Is creation incomplete without God's continually sustaining it?

2 If so, when is it complete?

3 Does that completion require other creative acts?

4 When asking '*How* does God's action operate in history?' can we expect an answer?

5 What does intervention mean if we do not know how to explain it?

6 To what extent is natural and human activity independent?

7 Does consideration of the ideas of cause and effect help us to understand the idea implicit in the belief in God's providence?

8 If God is transcendent, how can he also be immanent? If God is above the universe, how can he be active within it?

VI

EVIL

1 Explain dualism

2 Why do Christians reject dualism?

3 Or, Do some Christians accept a form, or forms of dualism?

4 What are the two sources of evil. How do we distinguish between them?

5 The world has its independence of God. Does this involve a form of dualism?

PART II

7

CREATION:
THE THEOLOGIAN AND THE SCIENTIST

Introduction

We now set out views as to what constitutes a theological statement of the doctrine of creation. In doing so we state how the theologian considers the province of the scientist and the status of the scientist's statements. What is distinctive about what theology says about origins? Can the theologian be in conversation with the scientist over the doctrine of creation?

A brief word about the terms 'theology', 'theologian'. We use these terms in the broadest sense possible. Theology makes statements in the name of faith. Sometimes these may be directly related to matters of faith. Sometimes they may be made because they are thought to be required by a belief or by a set of beliefs. Claims deemed to be required to explain faith or made in the name of belief, however simple, come within the orbit of the meaning of 'theology' The 'theologian', whether the writer of books or the simple believer, says 'This is my belief', and also 'This is required by my belief.' The simplest believer engages in theology.

A. The Distinction between Scientific and Theological Statements.

One of the very important challenges that comes to the theologians of the present time is that they should make clear what kind of statements they are making and should show how such statements have meaning, that is, that they should indicate the criteria by which such statements should be judged. This is a challenge with a two-fold significance. What are believers doing in the process of making theological statements? They are being asked for clarification of their assertions, if indeed that is what they are. They must defend the relevance of their statements. They answer by indicating how they arrive at their claims. They have both an apologetic and at the same time a methodological task.

In no small part, the fruitless discussions that have plagued the relations between science and theology have been due to methodological unclarity. If there is an elementary confusion as to what constitutes science, on the one hand; and on the other, what the task of theology is, good-will and honesty may be barriers to understanding rather than means to it. For both may feel that whatever they say is worthy of the same credence. When the scientist speaks as a theologian he may be a very bad or not very good theologian, and when the theologian makes scientific statements, he may not know why he has to be making such statements, or whether he has to be making them at all. It would be better to say that he may not know why (or even that) he is making scientific rather than theological statements. If the theologian does not realize that the hidden scientist is becoming manifest, or if he thinks that scientific statements are necessary to buttress theological statements, he may not be clear what constitute distinctively theological statements. And *mutatis mutandis* the same goes for the scientist.

We now illustrate this by reference to specific examples. Take the following statements: (1) 'The world is six thousand years old.' (2) 'Reality is material,' 'reality is rational'. (3) 'I believe in God, Maker of heaven and earth,' 'God created the heavens and the earth.' The first of these statements is the kind of statement that can be held up for the scrutiny of the physical scientist or historian since there are empirical tests which they can devise and apply to the body of facts about which the statement is concerned. That is to say, statement (1') 'The world is six thousand years old' is either true or false and can be shown to be such by examination of the evidence. Only purely scientific considerations are necessary for the scientist to arrive at his conclusion. Even if he believes the statement on other grounds than scientific ones before the evidence is available, he cannot claim scientific certitude for the belief. If he believes statements on other than scientific grounds, the claims can only function as hypotheses. They will then be verified or falsified.

If, however, such an hypothesis is made the ground for theological statements, and it is shown to be false the theologian is in trouble. A hypothesis proved invalid as a means for fruitful scientific research, by its failure at 'expansibility,'[24] will, or should, cause a crisis in the theological foundations. The alternative is obscurantism which may take various forms. One may deny the correctness of the scientist's statement, contest the methodology of the scientist by which such a conclusion was reached, or claim that the statement is not scientific at all but theological, perhaps even religious. This attitude, in short, is one of entrenchment. We know that a theory about the cosmos that fails to explain the known facts cannot serve as a foundation or support for a worthy theology. One that succeeds may.

The task of theology is distinctive. That means that it does not hold its domain in fee to the scientist. The task of the scientist is distinctive. He does not have to consider the statements of the theologian as binding upon him, although he may if he wishes take the purported scientific statements of the theologian as hypotheses to be tested according to his own distinctive methods. He will then pronounce them true or false, according to the evidence. It is

24 The term is Frederick Ferre's. Cf. *Language Logic and God* (London: Eyre and Spottiswoode, 1962), Chapter 10.

obvious that the theologian has nothing to fear from the scientist, provided he sticks to his job as a theologian. But he must certainly have methodological clarity if he is not to fall into elementary confusions and engage in nervous and fruitless argument, or produce unwarranted dogmatism that renders both altercation and discussion impossible. Where there is argument there is at least life. The case of Galileo became a classic example of an imposed and recalcitrant dogmatism.[25]

Since the nineteenth century, conflict between religion and science has found expression in Christian fundamentalism and the

25 We must not overlook the possibility that a cosmological scheme can be raised upon false statements, i.e. bad science, or what purportedly claims to be scientific. A cosmological scheme set forth as philosophy, or accepted by theology, would be overthrown if the bases upon which it rested came within the province of science and were shown to be false by scientific research. This has caused much of the trouble between scientists and the church in the past. When in earlier days a geocentric scheme of the cosmos was the basis for a theological system, a wrecking of the geocentric foundations demolished the rationale of the theological system.

'The fact that science has logical and anthropological questions and the fact that these scientific judgments have won almost universal acceptance at the expense of the corresponding theological propositions have done much to discredit the whole theological enterprise . . . The oft-repeated pattern of response on the part of theology in the face of empirical data which goes contrary to theological expectation is first to reject and attempt to suppress the offending information; when that becomes impossible, to construct ad hoc explanations to account for the information; and, finally, to announce, It really wasn't an essential point of doctrine. It is little wonder that after a series of such events a general suspicion should arise that theology lacks any valid method of justifying its claims.' E. Ashby Johnson, *The Crucial Task of Theology.* Richmond: John Knox Press, 1958, p. 37.

theory of evolution, and has focussed on the question of the age of the earth. The following statement makes clear that such opposition is quite unwarranted. What it says is that an evolutionary theory that eliminates the distinction between man and animal is based on faith and so is not scientific.

> Science can conflict only with science, and faith only with faith; science which remains science cannot conflict with faith which remains faith. This is true of scientific research, such as biology and psychology. The famous struggle between the theory of evolution and the theology of some Christian groups was not a struggle between science and faith, but between a science whose faith deprived man of his humanity and a faith whose expression was distorted by Biblical literalism. It is obvious that a theology which interprets the Biblical story of creation as a scientific description of an event which happened once upon a time interferes with the methodologically controlled scientific work; and a theory of evolution which interprets man's discordance from older forms of life in a way that removes the infinite, qualitative difference between man and animal is faith and not science.[26]

That 'interference' would mean a radical revision of the definition of science. The believer often does not realise how far reaching the implications of that revision would be when they make the suggestion with apparent ease and unconcern.

The philosophical statement, (2) 'Reality is material' is different from the previous example ('The world is 6000 years old'). However the issue is settled in this case, whether the proposition is affirmed or denied, will not affect the ongoing labours of science. Anyone making this statement may well make it in view of the success of the methods of the scientists and may take into account

---

26 Paul Tillich, *Dynamics of Faith*, pp. 82-83.

its very success as one of the prominent considerations. So also would one who denied the proposition and asserted the counter-proposition, 'Reality is rational'. Affirmation or denial of the philosophical claim does not render either the theologian or the scientist supernumerary. Non-scientific considerations have been taken into consideration in framing the philosophical statement. Should scientists wish to deny or affirm it, they would have to pass beyond the bounds of their science and become — for the nonce — philosophers. And a very good scientist can become a very poor philosopher.

We have spoken of the scientific and the philosophical statement. Let us now turn to examples (3): 'I believe in God . . . Maker of heaven and earth,' 'God created the heavens and the earth.' These are theological statements. The statements are not identical, but they are both *confessional*. They are both statements about God and have their origin in the mind of one who believes in God. The form of the latter statement ('God created') may suggest that it is a statement about God only, while the form of the former ('I believe') may suggest that it is a statement about the believer only. The believer intends it to refer to what is not himself, even while recognizing that he is the one making the statement and making it as a believer.

The confessional statement, however, may seem meaningless rather than false. Such criticism rightly recognises that there is a distinction between the scientific statement and the theological statement, but wrongly devalues the theological statement because it cannot be proved or disproved by such empirical considerations as are available for confirmation or falsification of a scientific statement.[27]

---

27 This is the approach taken by the positivist who, in attempting to justify the empirical method of the scientist, extends the criterion of meaningfulness employed by the scientist to a general criterion of meaning. Language about God, since neither analytic or synthetic, is meaningless. It expresses the emotion of the subject or

Theologians have been quick to realize that no defence could be made to such an attack unless a basic distinction was made between the theological and the scientific statement.[28] Such a distinction is quite justified.

---

the subject's intention to follow a way of life.. The conflict between religion and science is ended once and for all.

'It is worth mentioning that, according to the account which we have given of religious assertions, there is no logical ground for antagonism between religion and natural science . . . . For since the religious utterances of the theist are not genuine propositions at all, they cannot stand in any logical relation to the propositions of science'. A. J. Ayer, *Language, Truth and Logic*. London: Victor Gollancz Ltd., 1962, p. 117.

The way to dispense with theological statements is to deny that they have any cognitive status whatever.

28 Cf. Paul Tillich, *Systematic Theology*, Vol. I. Chicago: University of Chicago Press, 1959: The question of the relation of theology to the special sciences is an aspect of the relation between theology and philosophy since the 'point of contact between scientific research and theology lies in the philosophical element of both, the sciences and theology' (p. 18). There is no direct point of contact between science and theology. Thereafter, Tillich makes three distinctions between philosophy and theology. (1) The first is a distinction in cognitive attitude, between a 'detached objectivity' and a commitment, an involvement in the content which he is expounding. (2) The second is a difference in the respective sources: the philosopher looks at the whole of reality to discover its structure within that whole; the theologian looks at the concrete reality of the church. 'The concrete *logos* which he (the theologian) sees is received through believing commitment and not, like the universal *logos* at which the philosopher looks, through rational detachment.' (p. 24). (3) The third difference is a difference of content. They may speak about the same object but, even so, they are talking about something different. The philosopher deals with the categories of being in relation to the material which is structured by them.

If theologians would busy themselves with their business no problem would arise. The theologian has enough to do without making pseudo-scientific statements that neither he nor anybody else can defend. He does not have to make such statements. His task is to expound the fact of God's revelation. If wisely done, no objection by science will cause him to retract fundamental statements, one of which is that God is Creator. What does the scientist have to tell the theologian concerning the relation of creation and time, creation and history, creation and saving history? The function of science is limited to concerns about nature. To pass beyond nature as the point of reference of science is to pass beyond the boundary of science.

A further question concerns the relation between scientific statements and historical research. A claim concerning the age of the earth is an historical statement and so is amenable to proof by the kind of evidence which historians employ. Documents and artefacts give grounds for the dating of civilizations. By applying

---

He deals with causality as it appears in physics or psychology. He analyses biological or historical time. He discusses astronomical as well as microcosmic space. He describes the epistemological subject and the relation of person and community. He presents the characteristics of life and spirit in their dependence on and independence of each other. He defines nature and history in their mutual limits and tries to penetrate into ontology and the logic of being and non-being. Several other examples could be given. They all reflect the cosmological structure of the philosophical assertions. The theologian, on the other hand, relates the same categories and concepts to the quest for a 'new being.' His assertions have a soteriological character. He discusses causality in relation to a *prima causa*, the ground of the whole series of causes and effects; he deals with time in relation to eternity, with space in relation to man's existential homelessness. He speaks of the self-estrangement of the subject, about the spiritual centre of personal life, and about community as a possible embodiment of the 'New Being'. *Ibid.*

such methods, dates are established and appropriate relations constructed.

Such dating may be corroborated by scientific means: e.g. the carbon 14 method. While the theologian must be aware of historical studies, he is *qua* theologian not an historian. His particular job is not dependent upon the latest findings in historical research. If it were, he would have to wait upon the historian before he could settle problems or he would have to become an historian himself[29] and settle historical problems before he could make theological statements. A scientific statement is not a theological statement. Nor is an historical statement a theological statement. One may wish to claim that e.g. 'The world is 6000 years old' is an historical statement. It constitutes a claim. So it can be confirmed or disconfirmed by the varied testimony with which critical historians deal. Historians falsify as well as verify their constructions and conclusions. In this case they have produced plenty of evidence to show that the claim is false.

So the theologian qua historian may readily deny the claim. As we said of the scientific, so we must now say of the historical statement: it makes no difference to the theologian whether it can be verified by the employment of critical, scientific methods of historiography or not. Neither faith nor theology depend upon

---

29 An important distinction must be made here. It is between historical fact and the apprehension of historical fact. I may not be able to say as an historian that I have sufficient evidence to enable me to assert that such and such an event took place or such a state of affairs prevailed. It may be the case that it did. The problem for the historian is to show by historical methods that it did. A man may be a murderer, but to prove him such requires effort if it is to be successful. Even if one is convinced of it, there must be sufficient evidence to produce conviction. One involved in making such investigation may want to assert the event. on grounds other than historical. After all one needs an incentive to perform the often detailed research demanded in historical (and detective) work!.

such propositions. The implication is obvious. If the believer, in the name of faith, claims for whatever reasons what the historian or scientist pronounces to be false, he is refusing to understand. So he becomes obscurantist.

It has frequently happened that both scientists and historians have made radical changes when the evidence demanded it. If theologians depended upon them to make their own statements they would be entirely upset when the evidence led scientist or historian to revise their claims. There can be no such dependence.

We do not overlook the obvious fact that some historical considerations are relevant in that they establish that certain events took place, events which are a necessary, but not a sufficient condition for Christian faith.

B. The Uniqueness of Theological Statements Concerning Creation

We call attention to the fact that it is as Christians that we affirm the significance of *creatio ex nihilo*. We must therefore raise the question as to the particular way in which the Christian doctrine is elaborated. The Christian affirmation is confessional.

Different kinds of statements are to be clearly differentiated. Otherwise nothing but confused thinking will result. A confessional statement must not be confused with a scientific statement. Likewise a scientific statement is not to be confused with a theological statement. The *theological significance of* the assertion that God is Creator is not dependent upon scientific discovery or research. It is not the product of such discovery and research nor is it upset by it. It is the task of the theologian to answer the question, 'What is the significance of *creatio ex nihilo*' for the believer?' 'How old is the world?' is a scientific (or possibly an historical) question. The answer given to the latter question is of quite a different order from and therefore should not affect the theological understanding of the meaning of *creatio ex nihilo*. In fact, it cannot affect it if the provinces are clearly distinguished. Historical and scientific statements depend on evidence. When the evidence causes scientists or historians to modify or change their statements, theology would be in a parlous state if it had to depend on, and had to await the outcome of, such investigations. Such embarrassment is by no means unknown to the believer!

It is important to draw a distinction between the *that* and the *how* of creation. Scientific research cannot touch the basic theological statement *that* God created the world, or that God created the world *ex nihilo*. Opinions vary about the *how*, whether it is even a topic of possible discussion. When the basic confession *creatio ex nihilo* is discussed the Christian theist agrees on the basic point: God is the final reality. His act initiated what is. At this level the field is the theologian's *only*. No considerations of a scientific nature can touch the theological interpretation of creation at this point. The physical scientist also has his questions about the how, but he is answering a different question, namely 'What, speaking from within the system of nature, can we say of the set of conditions which resulted in the origin of the universe?' The set of conditions are physical conditions, and are constituted by the entities with which physics deals. The quest is most fascinating, but not theological.

The basic issues involved in the *creatio* doctrine are theological or philosophical ones. Such are basic because for the Christian. The conviction of creation roots in religious experience, in the revelation of God in Jesus Christ effective in the faith of the believer. Because the roots of the creation affirmation are essentially religious, the basic problem is a theological one.

Philosophy sets before us alternative explanations of reality The history of philosophy gives us a set of metaphysical systems which, if their 'first principles' (*archai*), are accepted, give an account of reality. Discussion between an idealist and a materialist on specific issues, e.g. the problem of the identity of a human being through space and time, or of the possibility of abstract thought, or of immortality, or of miracles, will constantly refer to basic postulates accepted as starting points, in terms of which the whole discussion is to be understood.

The Christian, as philosopher, enters the lists of philosophy and by the employment of reason alone, and with certain philosophical premises, *archai*, as his starting points, attempts to indicate a philosophically acceptable view of reality. While his premises are rational ones, the reason for the choice of those premises, and not others, may well be derived from non-philosophical sources. In this, the Christian who attempts philosophy is by no means unique. But philosophically the discussion must proceed on the grounds of philosophy, i.e. reason alone. The canons of rationality apply with all their force here.

The point of all this is a simple one. For the Christian the starting point is faith in Jesus Christ. A choice of metaphysical explanation follows and does not precede this faith. But, as philosopher, there can be no talk of Christian faith. He is out on the philosophical ocean, and he must row with philosophical oars or, believing himself to be on firm ground, to change the figure, he must build his structure with philosophical blocks. Thus, should he wish to refute, or at least oppose a philosophical doctrine that would exclude a doctrine of *creatio ex nihilo*, he must do so *on philosophical grounds only.* But while doing so, this does not affect his own basis — the Christian faith. The direction of the movement for the Christian is from revelation in Jesus Christ to a faith in God the Creator.

The essential Christian conviction is that God moved toward man and made his decisive revelation in Jesus Christ, that what is known of God is known in Jesus Christ, that in Jesus Christ we have the clue to the meaning of reality, not this or that part of reality only (although this as well), but to reality as such. This means that the Christian must attempt to see every aspect of reality in the light of God's revelation in Jesus Christ. We emphasize: the starting-point, the *sine qua non* of Christian theology is belief in Jesus Christ. Belief in Jesus Christ is evoked by God's revelation in Jesus Christ. That is given. Once present it is never questioned. The faith in Jesus Christ that is a result of God's revealing activity in Him provides the theologian with the starting point. All Christian doctrine, works from this starting-point, A Christian doctrine of creation must start here. No scientific research or discovery can touch this basic religious conviction or its theological expression. It is a method of interpreting the world and an explanation of the very existence of the world. It is an explanation of the world that says basically that the world is dependent on a reality that may not be known by an examination of the world alone.

C. Representative Theological Statements of the Doctrine of Creation.

We now illustrate the observations made in the earlier part of this paper by referring to a few representative theologians.[30]

---

30 Theologians ask specific questions and deal with quite specific problems, for example: the relation between the present existence of man, and man as depicted at the creation. Conservative Theology, in treating the subject of creation, concerned with the account in *Genesis* 3 and the belief in what has come to be called 'the Fall', and generalising from it, is concerned not only with the problem of the coming into being of a cosmos. It connects the theme of the creation of 'Adam' (= 'man' = the human) with that of human nature. The question concerns the relation between the 'essential nature' and the present state of the human. Is man in his present existence different from what he was at creation? How shall we conceive the present 'fallen' i.e. sinful state of human creatures to their essential nature?

Different answers are given to this question in the name of theology. The Creator creates a being capable of 'sin', a creature with freedom, that may be misused.

(1) Literalist theology connects man's present estranged nature to a state of perfection before the Fall. Original man, Adam, was perfect, or—should we say— innocent. First there was innocence.

Then there was the expression of freedom. This constituted the 'Fall'. These stages were in temporal succession: first the innocence, then the disobedience, then the expulsion from Eden, then this sorry state of things entire.

(2) Non-temporal accounts of the relation find that such an account is incredible. Here differing answers are given, as illustrated in the theology of Paul Tillich and Reinhold Niebuhr. Tillich holds that there is a coincidence between creation and the Fall as illustrated in the following assertions:

Creation and the Fall coincide in so far as there is no point in time and space in which created goodness was actualised and had existence . . . . Actualised creation and estranged existence are identical. Only biblical literalism has the right to deny this assertion. . . . Creation is good in its essential character. If actualised, it falls into universal estrangement through freedom and destiny. Paul Tillich, *Systematic Theology* I. Chicago: University of Chicago Press, 1959, p. 44.

Kenneth Hamilton comments on Tillich's presentation:

'Accepting Tillich's formula, then, does not mean identifying finitude and evil — even if this is escaped by the hair-breadth of a logical distinction ontologically meaningless. It does mean having to think of Creation and the Fall together as one complex making up the predicament from which we have to be delivered.' *The System and the Gospel*. London: S. C. M. Press, 1963, pp. 152-153.

(3) It is with this identification of estranged existence with the essence of finitude that Niebuhr takes issue. We can entertain the idea of human perfection. We recognise that we do not encounter such perfection in human beings, indeed not in ourselves. So how shall we think of the 'essential nature' of man. For Niebuhr, the character of the human is 'as a creature embedded in the natural order'. But the essential nature of the human also includes the freedom of his spirit, his transcendence over natural processes and finally his self-transcendence.' His conclusion is that 'sin neither destroys the structure by virtue of which man is man, nor yet eliminates the sense of obligation towards the essential nature of

Emil Brunner insists that the Christian can only speak of creation on the basis of revelation (12).[31] God, who 'alone *creates* the world by His Word . . . alone *imparts Himself* to man through His Word' (12), Thus the Creator means the God of the historical revelation' (5). Thus, the starting point for a Christian doctrine of creation is with the statements of the New Testament, not with the Old. To start with the Old Testament may lead to a violation of the basic principle of Christian theology: that all doctrines be related to Jesus as the revelation of the Father:

> The emphasis on the story of Creation at the beginning of the Bible has constantly led theologians to forsake the rule which they would otherwise follow, namely that the basis of all Christian articles of faith is the Incarnate Word, Jesus Christ (6).

This means that 'in principle our belief in the Creator is not bound up with the narrative of Creation in the Old Testament' (7).

When we start with the New Testament we find that there the concern is not primarily with the 'fact of Creation and the manner of Creation.' The New Testament is concerned with 'the reason why the world was created and to what end; while the narrative of the Creation in *Genesis* says nothing about this at all.' The Prologue to the Gospel of *John* is quite distinct in its approach.

> In the Prologue to the Gospel of *John* the Creation is mentioned in a way which we find nowhere else in the Bible; here it is clear that when a believer in Christ speaks of the Creation he means something different from 'explaining' why there is a world, or why things exist. In this witness to the Creation we are all addressed, and the meaning of our existence is

---

man, which is the remnant of his perfection.' Reinhold Niebuhr, *The Nature and Destiny of Man.* Volume 1. pp. 285-287.

31 References are to Emil Brunner, *The Christian Doctrine of Creation and Redemption.* Philadelphia: The Westminster Press, 1952.

defined. Here there is no question of confusing the
Creation with a cosmogony (8).

The love of God is the final cause of creation. The 'ideal reason'
for the creation is revealed in Jesus Christ. This is why the Old
Testament story of creation cannot be the starting point for the
Christian doctrine of creation (13).

Brunner insisted that the distinctiveness of a Christian doctrine of creation is that it finds the meaning of creation in Jesus
Christ. He also insists upon a distinction between the provinces of
science and theology, which we have previously described at some
length. We are to be well advised 'once for all to abandon the con-
temptible habit of taking refuge behind the hypothetical results'
(33) of natural science, 'this dirty trick of a lazy apologetic.' That
is not the way out of any sticky problem of theology.

> There are plenty of hypotheses left . . . and none
> of these scientific results affects ultimate questions
> at all. For, . . . these questions are only raised by the
> *narrative* of the Creation in the Old Testament, but not
> by the truth of the Biblical account of creation (33).

Faith does not set up a counter world-view which finds itself
in conflict with that of the scientist. God's action is not subject
to the control of objective observation. Once the theologian, the
believer, says it is, he has surrendered his case to the closed world
of the scientist *qua* scientist. 'The objects of faith cannot be proved
objectively.' 'Objects of faith . . . are apprehended as such only by
the eye of faith.'[32]

The world, the universe, may thus be 'explained' on two levels:
from the point of view of science which, as physical explanation,
concerns itself with the phenomena and from the point of view
of the believer who concerns himself with the purpose which he
finds that, in faith, the phenomena reveal. The distinction is abso-

---

32 Cf. Rudolph Bultmann, *Jesus Christ and Mythology*. New York:
   Charles Scribner's Sons. 1958, pp. 65, 69.

lute. There can be no contradiction between the two explanations, except the provinces be confused and the believer think that statements of faith are scientific explanations, and the scientist think that statements of science exclude the possibility and meaningfulness of faith.

This provides an illustration of the concern that the doctrine of creation be expounded theologically by the Christian theologian, and that he not become embroiled in needless, fruitless controversy over a question about which there can be no controversy.

There is broad consensus among theologians about the positions we have sampled here.

PART III

8

A CONVERSATION

Three Christian friends meet to discuss creation. Edward is a conservative who holds fast to the tradition. William is a sincere but somewhat puzzled believer. Harry has asked a lot of questions, listened carefully to suggestions and found some answers. Now he shares them. Then another friend Susan, the sceptic, joins them.

Edward

I believe God created the world in six days and that the world is about six thousand years old.

William

Ah! Yes! That has been the accepted teaching within the conservative tradition. But it is very difficult to square that with the verdict of so many scientists, anthropologists, and others who with good reason tell us that we need to allow vastly more time to explain the evidence. But I have a suspicion that when we focus on this question we are somehow missing the real point.

Harry

Let's ask Edward why he believes that the universe is so young.

Edward

It is required from the account in *Genesis* and by synchronising biblical genealogies with historical anchors. Since the Bible is our authority in these matters we may not, and do not, need to look elsewhere for the facts.

William

I find that very puzzling. Which facts are you going to say are settled because of the words of Scripture? Surely there are some areas about which Scripture has nothing to say, and certainly not in competition with our contemporary scientific understanding of the universe. The ancients simply had no idea of some of the basic concepts of contemporary science: light years, genes, electrical terms, to name a slight handful. They had no idea of the enormity of the universe, and would be at a loss to understand the millions of light years needed to explain its reach. Not to mention that they took for granted the framework of a three storied universe The heavens were above the earth. A subterranean world was literally beneath the flat earth. That is the way they thought about the universe. From their point of view on a flat earth, heaven was up. *Sheol* and *Hades,* Hell *was* below. It was literally the 'underworld.'

Harry

Then there is the question of history and the historical understanding of the past, and the establishing of past events on the basis of trustworthy historical methods. The conclusions of the historian must be taken into account. You can't simply say what events took place and what their significance was without examining and establishing evidence for your claim. Genealogies are not to be trusted for chronological purposes.

Edward

It is enough for me that the Bible is inspired and so has authority which must not be questioned.

William

Not even to ask the question, 'What kind of authority does the Bible have?' Surely you will acknowledge that this is a relevant, indeed crucially important, question. I do not think that I can accept that the fact that the Bible has authority guarantees that all its statements are literally true.

Harry

Indeed not. The Scriptures have to be interpreted. That means asking in each case about the character of the passage in question. Some passages purport to be accounts of literal happenings. Whether these are accurate will be tested by the historian who hopes to find relevant evidence. But some passages are not historical accounts. So then the question of finding, indeed even looking for, evidence to corroborate what is written is misguided. That is not the kind of authority that the Bible has. Nor can I accept your claim that the inspiration of Scripture guarantees its authority. That is a non sequitur But that is matter for another day!

Edward

But the Bible cannot err since it has God for its author.

William

I am coming to see that because the Bible has human beings as the source of its writings it is quite possible, even to be expected, that we shall find problems. What is clear is that all the various writings contained in Scripture have their own history. It is essential for an understanding of each writing to search for and, if possible, give an accurate account of how the writing came to be written and, where relevant, its relation to other writings, giving an account of its literary and historical context.

Harry

Please go on. Don't stop there William! Our next conversation might well be about the authority of the Bible.

William

There is something more which has puzzled me. I believe we touched on it a few moments ago. We have to discern whether in any particular case we should interpret the passage of Scripture literally. Is it an account of what actually happened, or does it point to a truth that lies deeper than a set of recorded events ?

Harry

Indeed! Let's think about the opening chapters of *Genesis* in the light of your remark. For, I think you have to agree that the first chapter is not to be taken as standing alone and to be made the almost exclusive focus of our attention. That is what seems to be happening when the age of the earth and the manner of creation (in seven literal days) is made the predominant theme. We must rather see that the creation story points to the reality of God the Creator. So our focus is not to be on this act and that act followed by another. But on the reality and being of God. We go beyond the act to the Creator and ask what the story tells us about him. It shows clearly that he acts in his independence, transcendence and freedom. But there is more. We see that the creation story points also and clearly to the reality of humanity, telling us about the human condition. Created beings are dependent, free, and fallen. Chapter three with its account of woman's and man's Fall completes the message. The first chapter is not to be read on its own.

William

OK. But there is also the second chapter. What do we make of the details?

Edward

Just take them as they are stated and imagine the events as told.

William

But it is a different account isn't it? If you say it is to be taken literally, then you must believe you can give details as to what happened. Don't tell me that you can't do that because the ways of God are different from our ways.

Harry

If it is a literal account then the language is what the scholastics called univocal. So God makes something, not out of nothing, but out of the ground, out of dust, dirt on the ground. Dirt being shaped. God breathing into the form so shaped. Man emerging with breath. Man having a rib taken, Woman fabricated out of the one bone. Literal? Univocal language?

William

There was something that I wanted to ask Edward. When you say that the narratives of the Bible are to be taken literally, doesn't that mean that you are going to accept the view of the world which the ancients had? When you say that the narrative is literal you are bound to say also that the view of the world that girds it as a framework is also to be accepted as true? I don't think that you can escape that, whether as a conclusion or an assumption. Perhaps you do not recognise that! For example when Joshua says 'Sun stand thou still!' that assumes an earth-centred universe with the sun moving across the sky. But you do not believe that. I am quite sure.

Edward

There are many things which I do not understand.

Harry

But there are a lot of things you do understand, and there are other things you could understand if you would only apply the things you do understand and think about what they imply, in this instance the relation between modern astronomy and an ancient text.

Edward

But surely it is a matter of giving first place to the inspired words of Scripture rather than to the pronouncements of human beings. So I do not hesitate to deny the ability of science to provide adequate alternative explanations.

Harry

Do you know anything about geology?

Edward

Not really. Do you?

Harry

I am not putting forth a theory to challenge the experts.

William

So you want science on your side, Edward, when you claim that confessing God as Creator binds you to saying that the world is young. So then you hope to find an alternative and equally plausible scientific explanation? If you fail in that endeavour, your whole pack of cards comes tumbling down. I mean, your account of creation is at risk. Don't you see that Edward? You are claiming 'An ancient book tells me that the world is young. An ancient book tells me that creation is instantaneous. So I must find my own scientific explanations to agree with these ancient accounts. That sounds like special pleading, making a confession rather than giving an account? So you try to give your alternative to the geological, biological and physical explanations given by the various sciences. That is neither scientific nor rational I am afraid.'

What do you say Harry? Do you want science on your side? Do you want to make a similar claim, namely that if you cannot square your account with science, or should I say square science with your account, so much the worse for science.

Harry

No! I shall accept what scientists say about the age and provenance of the world, since they have their appropriate way of providing answers to such questions. But I do this quite in independence of my belief in God as Creator. Since the two are quite separate spheres I shall not need to question the accuracy of the conclusions of science, nor doubt the fruitfulness of scientific theories. Their explanatory capacity is what counts. That is for me quite independent of my religious belief in God the Creator.

So I have no anxiety about the scientists, nor do I need to create alternative explanations to make them agree with mine. The two spheres are quite distinct. I do not need, and therefore do not get started with, a quite fruitless and unnecessary, not to say, illogically derived, task of challenging scientific conclusions and methods. If I challenge them it will be on the same ground as the scientist himself stands. Most creationists, I dare to say, do not have that competence. I do not engage in such activity because my faith is not threatened. Creationists do because they think that a challenge to their account of creation is a challenge to their faith in God, the Creator. This is the unfortunate consequence of such literalism.

Edward

I think that it is most unfortunate that you do not accept what I am saying.

William

Oh! Come now! What are you saying? That you can live with contradictory beliefs, recognising that they are contradictory. That you are at home with an ancient world-view while reading Scripture and live within a quite different world-view for the rest of your being and thinking? Or that you can bracket off, ignore science. But I have something else in mind. I can see what Harry means when he insists that we look at the meaning the creation account intends. It speaks of man's physical dependence on breath, woman's dependence on man, and dependence of the whole on God, without whose creative act nothing would be at all. It points to God freely creating. It points to God as other than the creation. Creation is not part of God. That is pantheism. Surely that is the intended message. I cannot see how Edward can take the account as if God were just like a human craftsman. For the human craftsman relies on the materials with which he has to work and is limited by the characteristics that those materials possesses.

Harry

There is a way of expressing the essential difference. It is to say that God's creation is 'out of nothing' (*creatio ex nihilo*). So let's consider how we can use language meaningfully of God. We say 'God creates'. Then we think of a human creator. We say that God is transcendent. That is how I understand the *Genesis* account. So we cannot say *how* God creates. We can only understand in terms of our own experience of humans making things. But then we make appropriate qualifications to enable us to speak with meaning about God. Then we claim that this says something comprehensible while at the same time denying that this is totally adequate when speaking of God creating. Our language about God is analogical That, I believe, preserves the required reticence when we make claims about God's activity. We do not trespass beyond the boundaries of our limitations. The ways of God transcend our limitations. God's transcendence refers also to our knowledge of God. To put it in technical terms, God's transcendence is epistemological as well as ontological. In simple terms, God's being is other than ours. Our knowledge of God is limited by that otherness.

Edward

So how can we speak of God at all if we cannot attain any adequate knowledge of God? We either speak literally about him or else we can say nothing at all.

William

But that is simply not true. There is a middle way between literal, univocal, language and equivocal language, the latter being the negative way of denying the relevance of all human attributes: God is not x, not y. not z. I've thought about that, but find myself in difficulty when I try to put it into words. And of course the Scriptures say a multitude of things about God. *Genesis* says that man is made in the image of God. Man is created in the image of the Creator. The word 'image' suggests there is some likeness between Creator and creature. So since there is some likeness, that likeness should enable us to say something from our human experience that has meaningful reference to God. So we do not have to be totally negative, but rather say that something in our experience is significant when we wish to speak about God. At the same time we do not say that it is literally and univocally true.

Edward

Why not simply start with the words of Scripture and take them literally? We know what judges are. So we know what God is when he is called a judge. We know what it is to be treated mercifully. So we know what God's mercy means. We know what human jealousy is. So we know what God's jealousy means. But I am getting impatient. Why don't we just stay with the creation account and just be content with a down to earth interpretation.

Harry

I am sorry to hear you say that. It takes a great deal of patience to arrive sometimes at an adequate understanding. You must be willing to suspend judgment, to bracket off your previously held ideas, at least for a while, and consider alternatives seriously. Meanwhile you read what you have not read before and exercise your judgment to come to reasonable conclusions. I do not want to get impatient with your impatience that can so easily lead to dogmatism and sometimes, dare I say it, to arrogance and fixedness of opinion. But I can see that when you say that we must start with our experience that can provide a road that leads to understanding. Of course we start with our human experience. But some of the aspects of our experience are more relevant than are others when it comes to speaking of God. So we must qualify what we say about God when we say he is judge. We must say that in some respects he is like human judges, Then we go on and say that in other respects he is not. This is the way of analogy. The language we use is our human language. But it is being used analogically, not literally in the sense of univocally.

As Edward says we know what judges are. So we can start there. Then we make appropriate denials of what we know about human judges. We make qualifications. We say, 'God is like a human judge, king, or father in these respects. He is not like a human judge, father, king in these other respects. So we are saying that not all the things we say of human judges can be predicated of God. There is both affirmation and denial. But that means we are not speaking 'literally' of God, in the sense in which Edward uses the term. But the preliminary question is about our choice of starting point. The Judaeo-Christian tradition has insisted that personal features are the right ones to employ. Western philosophical traditions have often chosen non-personal ones: Aristotle's substance for example. Remember the definition of trinity 'three persons in one substance', *tres persona in una substantia*.

William

Ah! Yes! The quest is sometimes a long one. I find that one step leads to another, but it all takes time. But unless we are willing to question and sometimes to suspend judgment, we remain at the same level with unchanged beliefs. I was once like Edward, impatient with ideas different from mine. But I gave myself a chance and I think that I am coming to a better and more satisfying understanding of the creation as a result, and of other things as well.

And look who comes here. Hello Sue. Want to hear what we have been discussing? Perhaps you have some ideas that might help us by alerting us to problems we have not discussed. We have been talking about creation.

Sue

So you have put the matter beyond controversy have you? Or have got stuck in arguing about the age of the earth when there is little to argue about?

William

I, for one, am very willing to listen to what you say.

Sue

Then you will know from our previous discussions, which have been both frank and friendly, and that is the way it should be, that I find the idea of creation at a point in time, if that is what you believe, impossible. It is a question of the method of approach. However you go on, you have to start with the world or 'universe' as it is. And it often takes an enormous amount of work to find out what the world is like. It has taken decades, indeed centuries of discovery, experimentation and thought.

Starting with the world as given you then ask for an adequate method of explanation. Or I should say for adequate 'methods' of explanation, for there are so many aspects that no one method will suffice. So we start with the physical universe. That is what the *Genesis* account proposes to talk about isn't it: 'the heavens and the earth'?

We explain the complex phenomena by developing various sciences. The physical world is the given. We search for adequate explanations. We simply are not interested in pursuing questions about the beginnings of things except as they bear upon our understanding of the universe as it now exists. We simply do not multiply explanatory principles, or what purport to be explanatory principles. The history of science has been the story of the abandonment of false ideas, unnecessary 'explanatory' entities, and misguided methods.

Our world is a wonderful world. But I am not really interested in stories about a transcendent creator who brought it into being and who at every moment sustains it in being. Why should I be? That goes beyond our limited ken and I am happy to accept the limitations of my understanding, if that is what you call it. Our propositions, theories, hypotheses, convictions, and methods have reference to the given world and we must stay within those limitations. All else is speculation. Sometimes we are wrong. But we welcome falsification. That is the road to progress in understanding.

William

I have no desire whatever to downgrade the work of scientists. Nor do I accept that because it is so often and characteristically theoretical it is not important. Theories are the very fabric and incentive of the scientist. What I struggle with is how to reconcile

the scientific account of the world with a belief in God as Creator.
What does Edward say about that?

Edward

It does not worry me at all. My belief is quite simple. Since
the Bible says that God created the world in six days, I take it to
mean that quite literally. Before the six days there was no world.
After six days there was.

William

I want to recognise the Biblical account also. But there is a
more reasonable argument than the one you have proposed.

Edward

I doubt it, but let me hear it. I think that I will have heard it
before.

William

You may have done. But you should give it your consideration.
It is one thing to hear. It is another to understand. Why not say
something that I know you believe because it is entailed by what
you have just said? Why not say more simply, Before God created,
there was no world. After the creative act, there was.

The *Genesis* account of the creative process is intended to focus on God as the free Creator, not to give a literal account of the
process. Taken as such it limits our vision of the majesty and sub-
limity of the Creator. It turns our attention to secondary matters.
So focus on the Creator.

Edward

I think that my understanding is the only shield against a
scientific theory which claims the world is billions of years old,
and also claims that it developed gradually into the present state.

William

Ah! Finally the problem has surfaced! I suppose you have had
that in mind from the start. So your explanation is really a negative one. The world could not have evolved gradually. To say so is

to dethrone God. Creation (a religious concept) and evolution (a scientific or philosophical concept or both) are at loggerheads. Is that what you mean?

Harry

Let's be clear about what Edward is saying. We cannot even consider a theory of evolution since the Bible, being true and authoritative, tells us that the world was created by the fiat of God in a few days. Is that it Edward? Are the 'six days' so important or is it that the 'heavens and the earth' were complete at a point in time past?

Edward

Yes that is right. The progress day by day to the completed creation requires that the world comes from God. What *Genesis* tells us is how that was accomplished. So we must find a scientific explanation of the facts as here given to us.

Harry

So you do not agree that understanding the creation story as it so beautifully points to God who alone, without struggle with rival deities, with no pre-existing material and out of his loving freedom brings a world into being, that all this makes irrelevant questions about when and how. Occupying ourselves with assertions about literal days and ancient views about the age of the earth we miss the majesty of the Creator before which we stand in awe. At most, such views could only have the status of hypotheses for the scientist. And hypotheses are helpful if they can be falsified.

Sue

Oh come now! Really! Edward, you must surely know what the function of a scientific theory is. It is to explain the observed data, to put the facts into some rational pattern. The pattern must be one that agrees with and explains our experience, observations, and experiments. The Big Bang theory and the theory of Evolution suggest explanations of enormous ranges of data, gathered with great effort over centuries of labour, examined with the greatest care and considered in the light of theoretical ideas some of which have proved fruitful, many of which have fallen by the way.

William

I now see that there is something wrong here, Edward. How can you declare that a scientific theory is to be rejected because an ancient document makes a claim about creation. As I see it now I have to argue:

The theory of evolution explains a vast amount of data.

The purpose of the *Genesis* story is not to provide an account of *how* God created, nor to explain those data. Rather the idea that God created is to be taken as pointing us to the transcendent being and activity of God.

Since that is so, it does not exclude scientific accounts. Nor does it conflict with such accounts. Therefore, taken in this proper reasonable sense, it does not conflict with what science says about the universe.

So I am not really interested any more to discuss the idea of a conflict with six day creation, coming out as the result of failing to see the real point of the creation story in *Genesis*. Certainly I am not going to fight with what the scientists have to say. Do you really think that I can ask them to agree to figure out the age of the earth from the ancient records of the patriarchs and not by consideration of the physical data? That sounds preposterous. I might observe that while *Genesis* talks about 'days' (mornings and evenings), we talk about billions of light years. The ancients had no idea of the speed of light, nor of the utterly mind-boggling vast extent of what they called 'the heavens and the earth.' They did not have the conceptions which centuries of thought and observation have produced. Let us not forget what happened to Galileo in Rome.

Sue

Bravo! A step in the right direction!

William

Is that what you say? But I think that I have taken more than your one step. Talk about God as Creator is religious talk. It is theological language. And, as I now understand it, there is no conflict between such talk and scientific language. So I do not have to confront scientific language as Edward does, but welcome it, for what it is — an outstanding achievement of human endeavour. I embrace it, and indeed shall, in good conscience, devote myself to scientific work if that is what I choose as my vocation.

Sue

So you are quite happy to say. 'Take the theory of evolution like any other theory in science, the theory of relativity for example, and let your understanding of the world be illuminated by it'?

William

Yes that is right. But I have to add that I do not do so with bad grace, always thinking that I am in some way calling into question my belief in God as Creator in so doing. As a layman and not a scientist I can rest assured that I can believe without being threatened by the pronouncements of science. I think that unless Edward takes a step or two in the right direction, he will not even be able to comprehend what I am saying. Most of us are not scientists and may not know the joy and satisfaction that comes from the illumination of experience by a scientific theory. And conversely, working scientists may not be aware of the issues we have been discussing, simply content with the routines of their scientific activity. Moreover, some scientists get carried away in their opposition to religious experience and belief, and must be reminded that opposition to religious belief on inadequate grounds is as indefensible as opposition to science on inadequate grounds. Dogmatism in the name of science is by no means unknown.

Sue

Quite, and theories that later were shown to be faithful were sometimes greeted not simply with opposition, but with ridicule, not only by believers, but by scientists working in the very field in which the new ideas were being suggested.

William

So you want science on your side, Edward, when you claim that confessing creation binds you to saying that the world is young. You find that ancient historians, geologists, anthropologists and others require a very old universe. So you take your task to be to find scientific explanation supporting your belief. You believe that without such a successful endeavour, your whole pack of cards comes tumbling down. I mean, your account of creation is at risk. Don't you see that Edward? You are claiming 'An ancient book tells me that the world is young. An ancient book tells me that creation is instantaneous. So I must find my own scientific explanations to agree with these propositions.' But this is neither scientific nor rational, I am afraid.

What do you say Harry? Do you want to make a similar claim, namely that if you cannot square your account with science, or should I say square science with your account, so much the worse for science

Harry

No! I shall accept what scientists says about the age and provenance of the world, since they have their way of providing answers to such questions. Then there are the historians' verdicts to consider as well. But I do this quite independently of my belief in God the Creator. Since we are talking about two quite separate spheres I shall not need to question the accuracy of the conclusions of science, nor doubt the fruitfulness of scientific theories. Their explanatory capacity is what counts. That is for me quite independent of my religious belief in God the Creator. So I have no anxiety about the scientist, nor do I need to create my alternative explanations to make them agree with his. The two spheres are quite distinct. I do not need and therefore do not get started with a quite fruitless and unnecessary, not to say, illogically derived, task of challenging scientific conclusions and methods.

If I challenge them it will be on the same ground as the scientist himself stands. Most creationists, I dare to say, do not have that competence. But I do not engage in such activity because my faith is threatened. It isn't.

William

So you and Sue are in agreement about your attitude to what science says about the world and the limits and range of what the believer says about creation.

Harry

Yes indeed. I agree with Sue that we should leave creation out of the range of the scientist and accept what science has to say about the world. As to the subject of God the Creator I will have to appeal to Sue on a different basis.

Sue

We'll leave that for another time.

Harry

I'll take that for a promise and look forward to that meeting and conversation.

READ THE COMPANION VOLUME

What a remarkable little book: at once a bold challenge to creationism, exposing its reactionary impulses and indicting its ideological abuses of the Bible; and, at the same time, a generous invitation for thoughtful Christians to celebrate the amazingly rich and varied portraits of creation, and thereby to bolster their faith in the Creator in a way that is both well-conceived and biblically based.

Terence J. Martin, Ph.D.
Professor of Religious Studies
St. Mary's College, Notre Dame

ALSO BY THE AUTHOR

Seldom does one read so thoughtful, so disciplined and so scholarly an account of the need to rethink the basis for the authority of Scripture in the Christian church.

James J. Londis, Ph.D.
Chair
Department of Humanities
Kettering College

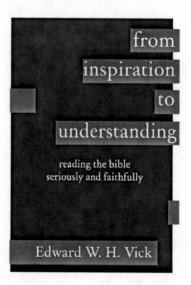

MORE FROM ENERGION PUBLICATIONS

Personal Study

Finding My Way in Christianity	Herold Weiss	$16.99
Holy Smoke! Unholy Fire	Bob McKibben	$14.99
The Jesus Paradigm	David Alan Black	$17.99
When People Speak for God	Henry Neufeld	$17.99
The Sacred Journey	Chris Surber	$11.99

Christian Living

Faith in the Public Square	Robert D. Cornwall	$16.99
Grief: Finding the Candle of Light	Jody Neufeld	$8.99
I Want to Pray	Perry M. Dalton	$7.99
Soup Kitchen for the Soul	Renee Crosby	$12.99
Crossing the Street	Robert LaRochelle	$16.99

Bible Study

Learning and Living Scripture	Lentz/Neufeld	$12.99
From Inspiration to Understanding	Edward W. H. Vick	$24.99
Luke: A Participatory Study Guide	Geoffrey Lentz	$8.99
Philippians: A Participatory Study Guide	Bruce Epperly	$9.99
Ephesians: A Participatory Study Guide	Robert D. Cornwall	$9.99

Theology

Creation in Scripture	Herold Weiss	$12.99
The Politics of Witness	Allan R. Bevere	$9.99
Ultimate Allegiance	Robert D. Cornwall	$9.99
History and Christian Faith	Edward W. H. Vick	$9.99
The Adventists' Dilemma	Edward W. H. Vick	$14.99
The Church Under the Cross	William Powell Tuck	$11.99

Ministry

Clergy Table Talk	Kent Ira Groff	$9.99
Out of This World	Darren McClellan	$24.99

Generous Quantity Discounts Available
Dealer Inquiries Welcome
Energion Publications — P.O. Box 841
Gonzalez, FL_ 32560
Website: http://energionpubs.com
Phone: (850) 525-3916

CPSIA information can be obtained at www.ICGtesting.com
Printed in the USA
LVOW040132110912

298237LV00001B/15/P